Obsession

Celebrities
and their
Stalkers

Obsession

Celebrities
and their
Stalkers

David Harvey

MERLIN
PUBLISHING

Published in 2002 by
Merlin Publishing
16 Upper Pembroke Street
Dublin 2, Ireland
Tel: + 353 1 6764373
Fax: + 353 1 6764368
publishing@merlin.ie
www.merlin-publishing.com

British Library Cataloguing in Publication Data
A catalogue record for this book is available
from the British Library

ISBN 1-903582-42-3

5 4 3 2 1

Cover Design by Pierce Design
Cover Image by Faye Keegan
Typesetting by Gough Typesetting Services
Printed by Cox & Wyman Ltd

Acknowledgements

There are a number of people who have been instrumental in bringing this project to fruition and I wish to express my gratitude to them and to those who gave up time to be interviewed, in particular, Rhonda Saunders, John Lawson, Paul Wright and Sarah Lockett. Les Kelly who collaborated with me on the 'Obsession' television series was most helpful with his time and advice.

Donal Campbell and Faye Keegan assisted with the design ideas and I must acknowledge the unfailing support of my colleagues Gillian Dwyer and Vanessa Kaminski.

Regina Looby provided me with a huge amount of research backup throughout the project and was always cheerful in her approach to some difficult assignments.

I would like to pay particular tribute to Chenile Keogh, Aoife Barrett, and all at Merlin Publishing. Their patience with an impatient and inexperienced author is much appreciated.

Most of all I would like to thank my wife Siobhan who really didn't have to take any notice of what I was doing for the past six months. She was busy giving birth to our beautiful son, Ben, but still took time to be interested in the 'Stalker' ramblings of her often inattentive husband. This book is for both of you with my love.

David Harvey

Contents

Introduction

Fame has always guaranteed money, attention and, it would seem in many cases, stalkers.

Recent incidents involving international superstars such as Madonna, Brad Pitt, and Steven Spielberg, have highlighted the problems facing the famous from over-zealous and sometimes obsessive fans – a pervasive and intrusive problem from someone who just won't go away. When the interest turns to obsession the results are often tragic.

Psychologists believe that the seeds of stalking are deep-rooted and that it only takes something small to tip a potential obsessive over the edge. The line between threats and actual harm is just as easily crossed. Many people believe that stalking is a phenomenon which only affects the rich and famous. In some instances, one might be excused for thinking that having a stalker has almost become a fashion accessory for those in the public eye. The frightening reality is that stalking is now as commonplace in 21st century society as other forms of crime.

Research carried out in the United States in 1998 estimated that one million women and 370,000 men are stalked each year. In the UK, figures up to April 1999 showed that more than 2,500 stalking cases had been brought before the courts; over a period of six months 1,250 people were found guilty and 165 people were jailed.

In most countries the seriousness of stalking as a crime is still grossly underestimated by law enforcement organizations. While attitudes are changing, stalking has only recently become a part of criminal law. In the United States, the lobby for the introduction of formal stalking legislation received a tragic boost in 1989 following the death of actress Rebecca Schaeffer. Twenty-one year old, Oregon born Schaeffer, was the star of the US daytime soap *My Sister Sam*, and had just appeared in her first film, when she was stabbed to death on her own front porch by an obsessed fan. Robert Bardo was the living embodiment of an obsessive nut. He was a school dropout who became a schizoid loner, living out his life in his bedroom, building a shrine to Rebecca. He couldn't have her so he didn't want anyone else to either; The Schaeffer incident led directly to the enactment of pioneering legislation in California, versions of which have subsequently been adopted by all fifty American states.

The California legislatures Penal Code Section 646.9 outlined the first legal definition of stalking anywhere in the world. It defines stalking as:

> '... the willful, malicious, and repeated following
> or harassing of another person, which includes
> a credible threat with the intent to place that
> person in reasonable threat for his or her safety
> or the safety of his or her immediate family.'

Schaeffer's murder also indirectly led to the establishment of specialist stalking departments within US police forces, the most forward thinking of which is the Los Angeles Police Department's (LAPD) Threat Management Unit. The TMU seeks to identify and manage stalking cases, providing intervention where appropriate and assessing risk in terms of the level of danger a suspect represents to the potential victim and the community at large.

Despite the adoption of this legislation the effect of a stalker's obsessive behaviour on the victim is still often not fully acknowledged, even by the victim's friends and relatives. Stalking is an invasive and often destructive act that can inflict long-term psychological damage on the victim. Stalking when taken to its most extreme form can even result in the victim paying the ultimate price of losing their life. It is a serious crime.

According to studies, almost anyone can become the victim of a stalker. In their 1993 study, Zona, Sharma and Lane stated that there were three main types or categories of stalker:

Erotomania is a stalking condition characterised by the simple, often delusional, belief that one person is passionately loved by another person. The obsessed person often goes to great lengths to get close to their idol or object of desire. Its manifestation is a serious medical condition classified as a subtype of delusional (paranoid) disorder known as 'de Clerambault's Syndrome'. According to Zona, Sharma and Lane, an erotomania stalker generally rejects any evidence, which might prove that their obsessive target is not interested. They can remain in a delusional state for years. There are very few reported cases of successful treatment for erotomania.

Love obsession stalkers demonstrate a condition not unlike erotomania where the obsessed person usually only knows their victim through the media but believes that they are loved by that person. The delusions are often linked to a serious mental illness, usually schizophrenia or bipolar disorder.

Simple obsession stalking is a condition where there

has actually been a prior relationship between stalker and victim. In cases of simple obsession the relationship has usually gone wrong or the stalker believes that the victim has mistreated them in some way. The 'wronged' person then stalks or harasses, seeking to either rectify the situation or looking for revenge or retribution of some kind. The revenge is intrinsically linked to the prior relationship between the parties.

There is now an increasing amount of academic, legal and psychological research being undertaken in this field. Experts are also promoting the need for a fourth category of stalkers, described as vengeance or terrorism stalking. This classification is radically different from the other three insofar as the perpetrators do not seek a personal relationship with their victims, rather, they use the activity of stalking to 'get even' with their enemies. No personal relationship need ever take place. In fact, the main desire in these cases is that one never does.

Building a character profile of a stalker is difficult, as many law enforcement agencies have discovered. Experts in the field believe that there is no simple way to classify the obsessive actions of stalkers – no way to pigeonhole their activities. The complexity of trying to build a comprehensive stalker profile is illustrated by examining the record of drug abuse or alcohol/drug dependency found in a large proportion of erotomania cases. The desire to behave in a violent or threatening manner towards an unsuspecting and undeserving victim is often a result of regular drug abuse by the perpetrator. Under the influence of drugs 'normal' characters, not usually corresponding to the profile of a stalker can be pushed over the edge. But there are some basic indicators which give an idea of the sort of person who gets involved in this form of extreme harassment. Stalkers with a simple or love obsession are predominantly female and heterosexual in orientation. In the case of simple or love obsession, a sexual preference other than heterosexuality, is rare. Whereas most stalkers with erotomania are male and over 40% of them are homosexual or bisexual. In many cases the stalker has been the subject of ongoing psychiatric attention for some time. Most surprising is that the average age across all three classifications is just thirty-nine-years-old. Overall, profiles dispel the commonly held view of stalkers as old men behaving as 'Peeping Toms'. As you will read in the following accounts, the modern stalker is a more sophisticated, more unbalanced and infinitely more dangerous individual.

In many cases, the acts of the stalker are a cry for help. Unfortunately their cry for help takes the form of an action that radically changes the life of his or her victim forever. This book does not set out to judge the stalkers detailed, or to analyse the life-changing effect on their victims. What I have set out to do is simply to tell eight stories of stalkers and their victims and to examine, in some way, the manner in which the attentions of over-zealous fans or admirers has led to years of pain, disturbance and, in some cases, death, for those they pursue. Apart from the presence of a persistent stalker in their lives, the subjects of each of these stories have another thing in common. They are, or were, all internationally famous celebrities.

If there is any conclusion to be drawn by this book it is that modern society promotes, and has adopted, a world of celebrity culture. In this world, people such as pop stars, sports stars, television and film stars and even football managers, achieve elevated status and become 'New Gods' to be followed and worshiped by each generation. For those with obsessive characteristics, ranging from the simply obsessed to persons suffering advanced paranoid disorders, these 'New Gods' continue to supply new targets for harassment, stalking and even death.

CHAPTER ONE

Beatlemaniac

'He walked past me and then I heard in my head… do it, do it, do it, over and over again…'

It was 11pm on a cold New York winter's night, December 8, 1980. In the shadows of a plush midtown apartment building a young man waited. He had already met his target once that day. He was now waiting in the hopes that he would see him for a second time. What unfolded in the next few minutes eliminated the icon of a generation and forever changed the way people in the public eye would live their lives. The young man was Mark David Chapman. He was waiting for John Lennon.

The worlds of stalkers and their victims do not usually collide by accident. Mark Chapman planned his journey to Manhattan to see John Lennon in minute detail. He even had two practice runs. Whether he planned to kill him on December 8 is a matter for conjecture. It may have just been an impulsive act. After all, he had met Lennon earlier in the day and could easily have done it then. What is certain, though, is that Mark Chapman knew what he was doing in New York. His presence there was the result of a long and tortured journey; one in which he lived more of his life in his mind than outside it; On the outside he was subdued, normal looking and respectful; On the inside lurked a maelstrom of emotion and contradictory thoughts. John Lennon and Mark Chapman were quite alike. In fact it has been said that if Lennon had met Chapman at some point in his career he would probably have liked him. Like John, Mark was a deep thinker.

Born on the May 10, 1955 close to Fort Worth, Texas, Mark Chapman was the eldest child of David and Diane Chapman. His father, an airforce sergeant, was discharged from the service shortly after Mark's birth. Following a university degree David Chapman moved his family to Decatur, a small town close to Atlanta, Georgia, where he had got a job with the American Oil Company. In 1962 they had a baby girl called Susan.

While the Chapman family life appeared to be normal by American 1960s standards, evidence suggests that Mark was not an average boy. He had the same interests as other boys but there was always something strange about him. Later he would tell psychiatrists that his childhood was a very unhappy one and that he was the sort of person the others would pick on. In a statement to his doctors he remembered that the other boys called him 'pussy'. This inevitably contributed to his habit of withdrawing into himself and spending time alone in his bedroom. Not being able to form relationships with boys of his own age he resorted to imaginary friends to prop up his solitary existence. Jack Jones, the author of *Let me take you down*, a biography of Chapman, described Mark's later comments on these fictional companions.

> 'I used to fantasize that I was a king and I had all these Little People around me... I was their hero and... I was on TV every day... they all kind of worshipped me... It was like I could do no wrong.'

It seems clear that Mark's belief in the unhappy nature of his family surroundings was unfounded. David

Chapman tried hard to include Mark in family outings but with limited success. David was a scout leader and was involved with the YMCA. He included Mark in everything, even teaching him to play the guitar. Despite a relationship that appeared to be loving and stable from the outside, Mark was later to tell psychiatrists that he hated his father. In one interview with psychologist Lee Salk he admitted that while his father spent time with him, he was never there for him emotionally. *'I don't think I ever hugged my father. He never told me he loved me, and he never said he was sorry – one of those guys.'* For Mark, his imaginary friends would always take precedence. His solitary life meant that he kept the outside world and his family at a distance.

In 1969, as a fourteen-year-old freshman at the nearby Columbia High School, Mark began to experiment with drugs. Mark was exposed to the hippy drug scene at the height of its popularity. He started using marijuana and soon moved on to LSD and any other hallucinogen he could get his hands on. He became defiant, ignoring his parents, growing his hair and staying out late. Highly impressionable and keen to impress, he fell in with a new drug-using crowd. They might have been viewed as freaks but they gave Mark a sense of belonging and a new rebellious personality. Locked in his room by his parents, he removed the door from its hinges and left the house, refusing to return for a week. At one stage he left Decatur for Miami, staying there for two weeks and living rough on the beach with other 'non-conformists'. When the money dried up he went home using a bus ticket bought for him by a responsible stranger. Mark was on a drug-crazed roll and according to Jack Jones it was the drugs which first made Chapman aware of the fury boiling inside him. Jone's quotes Chapman as remembering:

I was never one to sleep while doing acid, so I remember I was standing up in the room and everybody else was lying out, passed out on the bed. And I remember... there was a knife in the room. Something in me, while I was tripping... was trying to urge me to pick up the knife and stab it into these guys, into my friends. And I, of course, I had freedom of choice and I didn't do it. But it was a compelling urge to pick up this knife and kill these people. This is how these things happen when people are bombed out on drugs. They open themselves up to the bad elements of a spiritual nature and can be influenced to a point of doing some very damaging disastrous things. Thank God I avoided doing that. But I remember getting this urge.

In 1971, just as Mark's rollercoaster lifestyle was beginning to get out of control, he slammed on the brakes. A friend persuaded him that a Presbyterian prayer retreat would be a good place to meet girls. Mark decided to go along. He met Jessica Blankenship a girl he'd known from school. He also had a spiritual meeting with God. This was the first time he had come into contact with a spiritual being other than those he had imagined in his head. It had an intense effect on Mark. His appearance changed radically along with his beliefs; the long hair and scruffy, unwashed appearance disappeared, as did the drugs. With the fervour associated with a new convert, Mark threw himself feet first into Born Again Christianity. His new appearance – short hair, neat look, with a quietly spoken demeanour – was regarded by some as irritating but it was far preferable to the aggressive personality of Mark

Chapman the 'Druggie'. Mark was becoming normal again – normal that is compared to the abnormality associated with his drugs period. His new philosophy was to do 'good' and reject 'bad' or 'evil'. He saw himself as a bad or evil person during his drugs phase and everything that he did then was bad; everyone he associated with was bad; every hero and role model that he had previously worshipped was now bad. Mark rejected evil and adopted good. He removed anyone associated with that period from his orbit. John Lennon appears to have been one such association.

No teenager growing up in late sixties America could have failed to be impressed by, or at least have noticed, *The Beatles* and their music. Their songs had certainly affected Mark Chapman. He included many of *The Beatles* classics in his guitar-playing repetoire. John Lennon was a hero, particularly to the hippy youth of the United States. If John Lennon could tell the establishment to 'fuck off', well why couldn't they. To 'druggie' Mark, Lennon's antics were music to his ears – break the rules, grow your hair, reject convention and take drugs.

Over the years *The Beatles* music had changed. Their later output had become significantly more complex. Catchy, simplistically innocent titles such as *She loves you* and *Can't buy me love* had been superseded by songs with more depth and contemporary influences such as *Lucy in the Sky with Diamonds* and *Strawberry Fields Forever*. *The Beatles* had got into drugs, and had sought the advice of eastern spiritual leaders. In a typically irreverent interview for the *London Evening Standard* in 1966, John Lennon famously declared: 'We're more popular than Jesus now; I don't know which will go first – rock n'roll or Christianity.' In the United States the comment led to a hate campaign directed towards *The*

Beatles and John Lennon in particular. The anti-Lennon feeling was most acute in the deep-south American 'Bible Belt' where burning *The Beatles'* albums became the fashion of the month.

It's clear that upon finding God, Mark Chapman began his rejection of John Lennon. It was a rejection but not to a degree where he would have been prepared to kill him. At this point he only went as far as persuading his high school prayer group to sing his version of *Imagine*. He replaced the main lyrics with, 'Imagine if John Lennon was dead'. Mark's attitude to Lennon at this point could be described as passive dislike rather than hatred but he was storing up resentment against the singer and his beliefs for another day.

Lennon was just one of the many things that Mark was moving to one side as his new found security and sense of identity increased. Since Mark had rejected Lennon he needed to recruit some new heroes. He found a new musical hero in Todd Rundgren. Philadelphia born Rungren was one of the mot eccentric musical talents of the early 1970s. His unusual style attracted a hard core following and he later went on to achieve international fame as the producer of the multi-million selling Meatloaf album *Bat Out of Hell*. Mark often spoke of the 'Gospel according to Todd'.

At this time Mark also discovered the figure who was to become the most important hero in his life. In this hero he could see much of himself, his anxieties, his emotional deficiencies and his problems. Michael McFarland, a member of Mark's Christian rock group, told Mark that he should read J D Salinger's *The Catcher in the Rye*. In Salinger's sixteen year-old angst-ridden protagonist, Holden Caulfied, Mark had found his hero. He identified almost completely with Holden's world-view – most especially his obsession with 'phonies'. Chapman later stated that he believed this book led him to murder John Lennon.

Mark went on to recommend *The Catcher in the Rye* to other members of his new Christian family. This group was rapidly replacing his real family and providing the support system the disjointed, misfit teenager needed. As his Christian activities intensified, his schoolwork and general demeanour improved. He became involved with the South DeKalb branch of the YMCA where his father was a scout leader and taught guitar. These changes were just more indications of the about turn in Mark's life. In his 'druggie' phase he wouldn't have been seen dead at the 'Y'. In his new Christian phase he was made Assistant Director of the summer camp and began what would prove to be a long association with the organisation.

Tony Adams, the former executive director at South DeKalb YMCA, believed Mark had 'real leadership abilities' and described him as a 'pied piper with the kids'. They called him 'Nemo', apparently after Captain Nemo in Jules Vernes' novel *20,000 Leagues Under the Sea*. When he won the award for 'Outstanding Camp Counsellor' the children stood and cheered 'Nemo, Nemo'. Mark was apparently delighted. There is no doubt that these were happy years for the teenage Chapman. He'd found a group of adults, children and even fellow teenagers that liked and respected him. He had status and influence and a future.

In 1973, Mark graduated from Columbia High School and moved to Chicago with his friend Michael McFarland. They tried to pursue their entertainment ambitions in Christian venues in the area. Mark played guitar while Michael lampooned political figures. The act *McFarland and Chapman* didn't last long and Mark was soon back in

Georgia working part-time at the YMCA. He also enrolled in a number of courses at DeKalb Community College to get a degree that would qualify him for full-time employment at the YMCA. As a reward for his hard work the YMCA chose him to participate in an international 'mission' to Beirut in Lebanon.

The Middle East in the early 1970s was no place for a group of American Christian teenagers. The 'missionaries' were quickly packed off back to the United States. Mark was offered an alternative placement at Fort Chaffee, Arkansas, working with Vietnamese refugees. Again the experience was a positive one for Mark. The Vietnamese loved him and he derived the same sense of belonging he had got from his involvement with the children of the summer camps at Camp Koda, as the South DeKalb programme was known. His bosses liked him too and respected his work ethic – he would often work double the required hours.

Fort Chaffee also introduced Mark to a new experience – sex. But his first sexual experience wasn't with his long time sweetheart Jessica Blankenship. Mark lost his virginity to his female roomate at Fort Chaffee. Their relationship had begun innocently enough but soon became physical. When Jessica, whom Mark regarded as his fiancé, came to visit him at the refugee camp he was guilt-ridden but couldn't tell her what had happened. This was the beginning of another bout of depression and self-doubt for Mark. His failure to confront Jessica and deal with issues scared both of them and triggered a downward spiral for Mark.

By the end of 1975 almost all of the refugees at Fort Chaffee had been located with families and the programme was ending. Mark's friend Dana Reeves drove from Atlanta to pick him up. As camp colleague Rod Riemersma, quoted in *New York* magazine in June 1981, remembered, Mark said:

> 'We're all going to get together again. One day one of us is going to be somebody. About five years from now, one of us will do something famous, and it will bring us all together.'

After leaving Fort Chaffee, and in the hope of getting a college degree, Mark spent a short period with Jessica at Covenant College, a strict Presbyterian college in Tennessee. He'd enrolled on the same course as her and encouraged the two of them to study together every night. When he had been at Fort Chaffee her visits had been the central part of his life and he had talked about nothing else to his camp colleagues. Meeting Mark every day became too much for Jessica. He left Covenant after one term and shortly afterwards Jessica broke off their engagement.

Mark went back to Decatur and was made Assistant Director of the holiday programme again, remaining there for most of the summer of 1976. A month later he quit his job after a row with one of the camp directors. His life was falling apart again. Like Holden Caulfield, he was '…standing on the edge of some crazy cliff.' His mood became depressive and suicidal; he considered himself a failure.

He'd started to put on weight, over thirty pounds in three months, and looked slovenly and unkempt. One day he'd been liked by everyone if not revered; the next he was jobless, loveless, felt worthless and had no status or direction in his life. It's clear that Chapman was considering suicide at this point. Somehow he got the idea that he should visit an exotic, beautiful place before ending it all – he chose Hawaii.

In January 1977 he checked into the most expensive and luxurious hotel he could find in Honolulu, *The Moana*. The accommodation was well beyond his means but lent him the air of a wealthy tourist and propped up his rapidly failing self-image. When the money ran out he checked into the YMCA. He was in a state of extreme depression. It's known that he called Jessica and tried to patch up their romance. Sensing his fragile mental state she played along but when he returned she left him in no doubt that their relationship was over. If nothing else, the trip home convinced Mark that he wanted to return to Hawaii – this time he wanted to go for good.

By May 1977 he was back in Hawaii, using the last of his savings on a one-way ticket to the island. With little money he was forced to stay at the YMCA again. He began earning existence money, working in the kitchens of a food factory. But the change of scene had failed to change his mental state and he became more depressed that ever. Believing that now was the time to end it all he spent hours talking to a suicide help line and planned his demise. He hired a car and having treated himself to a last meal of steak and beer, he drove to a deserted beach. He inserted one end of a vacuum cleaner hosepipe into the exhaust pipe of the car and the other end into the car itself. He switched on the engine, shut the windows and waited for death.

Some time later he awoke to the knocking of a man's hand on the window of the car. A passing fisherman had noticed his car and had stopped to see if he was all right. The hose had melted at the point where it was connected to the exhaust and the flow of carbon monoxide had stopped. Enough had entered the car to put Mark to sleep for a short while but no more. Studies show that to the majority of depressants the failure to carry out this 'average' suicide would have been yet another crushing blow; To Mark it was another sign from God that he had again been 'delivered'. He felt that God had given him the opportunity to lead a new life. He prayed for a chance to take advantage of it.

The next morning Mark turned up at a mental health clinic nearby. He had visited there once before and been prescribed medicine (which he'd thrown away). The psychiatrist he saw immediately recognised the symptoms of a severe manic depressive and admitted him to the Castle Memorial Hospital. Despite being placed on suicide watch for the first couple of days Mark was discharged within two weeks and was placed by the hospital in a job at a nearby petrol station. In a move reminiscent of his days at the YMCA, he applied for, and got, a job at the hospital he had just left. As the new maintenance man at Castle Memorial he was hard working and popular. Mark was back in business and his self-confidence was high again. So much so that he was ready to make another move – in the spring of 1978 he announced that he would travel again.

Mark decided on a round-the-world trip. His travel agent was a Japanese-American woman called Gloria Abe. They began seeing each other. What began with Mark sending thank you notes and little presents to Gloria for her kindness during their business dealings ended with Gloria arriving at the airport at Honolulu to see Mark off on his trip. They kissed and Mark promised to write to her everyday.

Chapman's YMCA connections meant cheap or even free accommodation wherever he went. He visited a number of countries in south-east Asia before returning to Atlanta via Geneva, Paris and London.

In Geneva he spent time with David Moore, a man who had been something of a mentor to him during his time at the YMCA. Moore later commented that he noticed a considerable improvement in Mark's temperament and mental stability at this time. The Atlanta visit could be interpreted as an effort to catch up on family and friends. In reality there wasn't much catching up to do. His parents' fractious relationship had fallen apart and now that his sister was almost grown-up they saw no reason to continue living together and had separated. Whatever 'friends' had been around ten years earlier had moved on. In reality, Mark was alone, and with support systems like the YMCA no longer available to him, there were few options left. If he had considered staying in the Atlanta area to try and rebuild his life there, he was soon under no illusions about how impossible that would be. There was nothing there for him. He decided to return to Hawaii.

On his return to Honolulu Gloria was waiting for him at the airport. As the relationship developed Gloria converted from Buddhism to Christianity. They married on June 2, 1979. Mark had resumed work at Castle Memorial, this time in the printing shop. Unlike his former job, where he would spend his days talking and mixing with people, the printing job was a more solitary occupation. On his own Mark had time to think – and thinking always led down the slippery slope to his depressive world. According to Mark, in his subsequent testimony to court appointed psychiatrists, it is around this time that the 'little people' returned in his mind.

Someone else from his past had also returned – his mother. Diane Chapman, now divorced from her husband, moved to Hawaii. This was bad news for Mark. While he'd enjoyed a reasonable relationship with Diane he'd spent the last fifteen years of his life trying to escape unhappy childhood memories. He was a new man now, a married man – a man with responsibilities. The last thing he wanted was his mother hanging around the place. Instead of shielding Gloria from his mother's intrusive presence Mark pushed Gloria into the front line. As a result the couple spent very little time together. Their time alone was also coloured by Mark's irascible moods and irrational behaviour.

The combined pressure of his mother's presence and Mark's sense of his responsibilities now forced him into making a series of life-changing moves. He decided that his printing job was beneath him and became the hospital's public relations manager. Despite his outwardly affable personality and ability to get on with people, public relations was not a skill Mark was cut out for and it proved a disastrous move. He also began to spend money to prop up his new lifestyle. They moved to a more expensive apartment. He began running up large credit card bills and he invested in works of art. Obsessive behavioural idiosyncrasies were always an underlying part of Mark's character. One Honolulu art dealer, Pat Carlson, told a journalist that she'd never seen anyone with such a new found obsession in art. She later commented, 'He would call me three or four times a week to talk about art'. He bought a Salvador Dali lithograph, *Lincoln in Dalivision,* for $5,000. Later he returned it and paid $7,500, some of it borrowed from his mother, for *Triple self-portrait* by Norman Rockwell. His behaviour was becoming even more erratic. He was moody and offensive, particularly to Gloria. When he was kept waiting one afternoon after he arrived to collect her, he stormed into her office and screamed abuse at her boss. When it happened a second time Mark ordered Gloria to resign – she duly complied.

Mark's emotional state and his finances were now in freefall. But, just as in the late sixties when the drugs were getting out of control, Mark did the unexpected – he slammed on the brakes.

In March 1980, Mark announced to Gloria that his next mission was to get them both out of debt. As with everything Mark got into, his debt reduction programme became an obsessive undertaking. He encouraged Gloria to scrimp and save every penny – naturally she obliged.

By the middle of 1980 Mark had been in Hawaii for three years. His quest to be 'set free' from his past, his problems and the 'little people' in his head had failed. He was in a marriage which he controlled but which he believed controlled him. His self-esteem, despite all the life changes, was at its lowest ebb. His thoughts were confused, his objectives hazy and his direction ill-defined.

In early September he wrote a letter to a friend, Linda Irish. He wrote 'I'm going nuts,' and signed off as 'The Catcher in the Rye'. Holden Caulfield's life, which he believed moved in tandem with his own, had once again begun to dominate his thoughts. He often drifted into the Honolulu public library and read a few pages of the book. In his mind Mark was becoming Holden Caulfield. Like Holden, Mark also hated 'phonys' and hypocrisy. He felt that no one really understood him and wanted to do something for which he'd be noticed. On one of his library trips he noticed a new book, *John Lennon: One day at a time*, by Anthony Fawcett. The book is a flattering, almost gushing, portrait of Lennon by his one time personal assistant. Rather than capturing Mark's interest, reading it generated a new rage within him.

For most of the seventies John Lennon was having a

difficult time. His acrimonious split from *The Beatles* had been mostly blamed on Lennon. His perceived selfishness and the influence of his wife, the Japanese artist Yoko Ono, had alienated many of his fans. His artistic work following the split had been patchy to say the least. Paul McCartney, his one-time songwriting partner had, eclipsed Lennon as a creative and commercial success. At Yoko's urging Lennon had become the figurehead for a number of peace initiatives and had baffled and bemused his fans with his 'bed peace' and 'hair peace' demonstrations. These protests brought Lennon to the attention of a very powerful group – the United States Government.

It was known that Lennon and his leftist friends were planning a national concert tour, which would combine rock music and anti-war activism. In 1972, the Nixon administration, fearful that Lennon's pro-peace, anti-Vietnam associations would adversely effect Nixon's chance of re-election, sought his expulsion from America. FBI Director J Edgar Hoover orchestrated an attempt by the Immigration and Naturalization service (INS) to have Lennon deported. A White House memo suggested that Lennon's US visa be revoked as a 'strategy counter-measure'. Lennon's protracted, and ultimately successful, appeal took three and a half years. He was granted permission to remain in the United States on the understanding that he kept his opinions to himself. Anxious to remain on American soil, he complied.

From that point forward Lennon had become something of a recluse. His life had also changed radically in other ways. In October, 1975 Yoko had given birth to their son, Sean. The three now lived in opulent surroundings on the sixth floor of the Dakota, a co-operative apartment building overlooking Central Park in Manhattan. Lennon spent his days looking after his infant son and gathering together thoughts and songs for his first venture into the recording studio after many years.

In 1979, John Lennon released *Double Fantasy*, a critically acclaimed album, reflecting the new peace and contentment he'd found in his life. Songs with titles such as *Just Like Starting Over* were melodic and spiritual and, it was claimed, biographical. Yoko, as always, was a critical part of this mix. The *Double Fantasy* cover featured a black and white photograph of the two of them kissing.

Despite her quiet demeanour, Yoko was a determined and ruthless driving force behind Lennon. She assisted in managing his business affairs and encouraged him to invest his money wisely. They now owned a significant property portfolio and bid on every apartment in the Dakota that came on the market, often topping all other offers by $30,000. It was also reported that John and Yoko had bought 1,600 acres in upstate New York and that they were breeding registered Holstein cattle. Not all of Yoko's ideas made sense. In an effort to spiritualise their lives Yoko had an ornamental oriental teahouse imported piece by piece from Japan. When they tried to put it back together it wouldn't fit in their apartment. Why no one measured it beforehand remains a mystery.

To Mark Chapman it seemed that John Lennon had sold out. According to Jon Wiener in his 1984 book, *Come Together – John Lennon in his time*, Chapman had, '…felt a sense of intimacy with John, and John personified his wishes, in ways that were distorted by his psychosis'. Weiner noted that, '…the court psychiatrist testified that he [Mark] idolised and adored this man. But intimacy is deeply threatening for paranoids, and Chapman was a true paranoid. … He decided that the man who represented his special wishes had betrayed him'. From being the iconic revolutionary with a vicious tongue and witty turn of phrase, John had become an Establishment figure with all the trappings – great wealth, fine surroundings, a lovely family and peace of mind. Mark felt that his music had also sold out. Gone were the agitating propagandist lyrics of the late sixties replaced with sentimental lyrics about Lennon's own life, especially about his newly-born son, Sean. In Mark's depressed state, John Lennon now stood for everything Mark and Holden Caulfield hated. He was a 'phony' and he must die.

On October 23 Mark quit his job as a security man, signing out for the last time as 'John Lennon'. By this time his money worries appear to have been dealt with. He sold the Norman Rockwell for $7,500 and his parsimonious attitudes of the past year had reversed his acute debt situation.

On October 27 he walked into J&S sales, a gun shop in Honolulu and spent $169 on a snub-nosed Charter arms .38 calibre revolver. He didn't buy ammunition from the salesman whose name, ironically, was Ono. He was afraid that if he were caught with a loaded weapon he'd be arrested. One can only assume that the police would have taken his possession of an unloaded handgun just as seriously – Mark's delusional mind didn't allow for this kind of distinction. He went home and told Gloria he was going to New York. As always she didn't question him. His mother, on the other hand, asked Mark if he was going to New York to do 'something funny'. She, like Gloria, had noticed the gradual deterioration in his mental state over the past months. Mark ignored her concerns. On October 30 he left Honolulu bound for New York and his destiny. Before he left he gave Gloria a copy of *The Catcher in the Rye* and told her to read it. He told her, 'It will help you to understand me better'.

Mark checked into the Waldorf Astoria in Manhattan and for a few days behaved like any other tourist. He befriended a number of women and entertained them to drinks and dinner. He also let it slip more than once that he was an important person in the middle of something big and that a major event was about to happen. He also spent some time at the Olcott Hotel, half a block from the Dakota building. The Dakota was like a magnet for Mark – he went there every day.

On his visits to the Dakota he chatted to the doormen. They saw him as just another harmless Lennon fan hoping for a glimpse of the great man. Despite Lennon's virtual anonymity in Manhattan, his recent spate of recording had attracted major attention. He was still John Lennon, a member of the greatest pop group of all time. A new Lennon album was big news. The release had attracted old Lennonites as well as a new breed of fans, too young to remember *The Beatles*, to the Dakota. The hardened doormen of the Dakota were among the most discreet in the city and wouldn't tell Mark if John and Yoko were in the building.

Whether or not Mark could have killed Lennon on his first visit to New York is a matter for speculation. He certainly hung around the Dakota for long enough. Maybe the right opportunity didn't present itself; maybe Mark just hadn't made up his mind. A technical difficulty had also arisen – he had no ammunition.

By the second week in November he was back in Atlanta. He stayed with his friend Dana Reeves who was now a Sheriff's Deputy. Mark explained that he needed ammunition for his gun to protect him from muggers in Manhattan. He said he wanted 'real stopping power'. Reeves obliged, supplying Mark with five hollow point cartridges. With no suspicion of Mark's real motives,

Reeves took him into nearby woods for target practice. Mark displayed a natural talent for marksmanship. If his mind was now made up to kill John Lennon, Mark wasn't telling anyone. 'If he had that on his mind, he did an excellent job of disguising it,' Dana Reeves later told a reporter from *New York* magazine. 'He put on a command performance. He was his old self of five years ago as far as I'm concerned.'

Mark also visited others from his time at the YMCA, all of whom said he was the 'same old Mark'. The true personality of the 'same old Mark' is difficult to pinpoint: outwardly friendly, respectful even, to old friends; inwardly tormented, visited constantly by his 'little people' and influenced by a fictional sixteen year-old boy to the extent that Mark believed that he had become the living embodiment of Holden Caulfield.

On November 10, Mark packed up his .38 revolver, now complete with ammunition, and headed back to New York. That night he went to see *Ordinary People*, the biggest film of the time. The Oscar winning movie tells the story of a well-heeled American family taking stock of their lives after their eldest son is drowned. Immediately after the film Mark rang Gloria in Honolulu. In an interview recorded shortly after his arrest, Mark said:

'… the experience in that Theater, somehow – when I called my wife, I had defeated, I had capped that volcano. And I called Hawaii and said, I'm coming home, I won a great victory. Your love has saved me.'

If Gloria imagined that her husband's mental salvation was at hand, the illusion was quickly shattered. Mark said:

'I told her I was going to kill someone and I
whispered – I remember whispering it in the
phone – John Lennon, I was going to kill John
Lennon. She said, "Come back", and that's
when I came back.'

Back in Honolulu Mark's mental condition deteriorated.
He continued to slide deeper into a delusional state. His
'little people' were talking to him on an almost hourly
basis, urging him on. Mark was tortured by John Lennon's
'phoniness'. He believed Lennon had betrayed not just
Mark, but the whole world. Mark felt Lennon was
behaving like a feudal emperor with his lands, his buildings
and his money.

Despite this growing determination to eliminate
Lennon, Mark led people to believe that he was changing
for the better. As a part of his self-enforced, and fictional,
attempt at rehabilitation he had made an appointment for
treatment at the Makiki mental health clinic for November
26. He never showed up.

A few days later he said goodbye to Gloria and his
mother and left Honolulu for the last time. It is hard to
believe that neither woman made it their business to do
something about Mark's behaviour and the danger he
might pose to himself or others, especially after his
comments to Gloria following the *Ordinary People* movie.
As far as she was concerned, Mark had come back from
New York for good. When he left again Gloria was either
too scared or too subservient to do anything against her
husband. His mother had clearly come to accept his bizarre
obsession with Lennon and his long absences. Neither
made any attempt to contact any medical services or the
police. In any event, leaving home was not a criminal
offence and the gun, which Mark carried, had been

acquired legally. The bottom line is that although Mark's mental state had deteriorated to the point of breakdown, no one could have foreseen the enormity of what would happen next.

On Saturday December 6, 1980 Mark arrived in New York. He told his taxi driver that he was a successful recording engineer who was on his way back to New York after a recording session with John Lennon and Paul McCartney. Mark then checked into the West Side YMCA where he'd stayed briefly on his last trip. Although he had several thousand dollars with him he was determined that his money would not run out before he'd completed his 'mission'. The YMCA is located on 63rd Street, just off Central Park West, nine blocks from the Dakota. It's a typical short-term low rental, hostel cum hotel.

Late that afternoon he walked to the Dakota, hoping to catch a glimpse of Lennon. He carried a copy of *Double Fantasy* under his arm. As he waited, he started to talk with two women, Jude Stein and Jerry Moll, who told him that Lennon would often stop and talk to them. Mark offered to buy them dinner if they would come back to the Dakota later. The matter was left hanging with the women non-committal about spending the evening in the company of this strangely intense Lennon fan. At around five o'clock Mark gave up and left the Dakota. Ironically the two women returned about fifteen minutes later and had a conversation with Lennon who was leaving at the same time.

Mark wandered around Manhattan until he returned to the YMCA. He was disturbed by the sound of two men in the next room having gay sex. Holden Caulfield had experienced the same disturbance in his hotel room in *The Catcher in the Rye*, when 'perverts' disrupted his stay. But while Holden was amused by the 'perverts' Mark was disgusted. He wanted to go into the next room and shoot them. However, he realised this would prevent him from completing his mission. To escape the perverts he moved hotel, checking out of the YMCA on Sunday morning December 7 and checking into the Sheraton Center at 7th Avenue and 52nd Street. He spent about three hours at the Dakota that day, his vigil coming to nothing. On his way back to The Sheraton he spotted John Lennon's face on the cover of *Playboy* magazine and bought it. It had an in-depth interview with John and Yoko. It was their first magazine interview for many years.

Everything he read in the interview just validated his opinions about John Lennon. The man he had held in such high regard as a teenager had changed. John was now a fat cat, a conformist and a member of the Establishment. He had sold out and become a 'phony'. One thing in the article particularly caught his attention. It mentioned that the Lennons often recruited staff from amongst the hundreds of fans who visited the Dakota. He thought that this would be a good way to get closer to John Lennon.

All alone in his room Mark was lonely, confused about life but sure about his immediate goal. His thoughts turned to Holden Caulfield. What would he do? In *The Catcher in the Rye*, Holden visits New York and calls a prostitute from his hotel room; Rather than have sex, the two talk into the night. Wanting to do the right thing, the Holden thing, Mark rang an escort service and asked for a prostitute. When she arrived, they just talked.

The next morning, Monday, December 8, 1980, Mark began to prepare himself. He built a 'shrine'. It appears to have included most of the main influences central to

Mark's 'mission'. Mark laid out his passport, a Todd Rungren tape, a photograph of himself with some Vietnamese refugee children and a poster of Dorothy and the cowardly lion from *The Wizard of Oz*, in a neat semicircle. Mark later said he laid out the Todd Rungren tape because he wanted to be regarded as a fan of a true genius and not of a 'phony' like John Lennon. The final and most unusual item was a bible, open at the page reading 'The Gospel according to John'. To the title Mark had added the word 'Lennon'.

As he left The Sheraton it dawned on him that he hadn't taken a copy of his own 'bible' to New York. Finding a bookstore nearby he combed the shelves until he found the familiar sleeve of *The Catcher in the Rye*. He tucked the loaded revolver away in his jacket pocket and held a copy of *Double Fantasy* under his arm. Everything was now in place.

Mark Chapman arrived at the Dakota before lunch. After a few words with the doorman, Patrick O'Loughlin, he leaned against the railings and began to read his book for the umpteenth time. He became so caught up in reading it that he didn't notice John Lennon getting out of a taxi and walking into the Dakota. A few minutes later Jude Stein, whom Mark had met on the previous Saturday, appeared. He offered to buy her lunch and she told him how he had only missed Lennon by a few minutes last Saturday. After two near misses Mark was determined to see Lennon this time. They walked back to the Dakota.

As they arrived a nanny came out clutching little Sean Lennon's hand. Jude, who had met Sean before, introduced Mark to the boy and the two shook hands. Mark later said:

He was the cutest boy I ever saw. It didn't

enter my mind that I was going to kill this
poor young boy's father and he won't have a
father for the rest of his life. I mean, I love
children. I'm the Catcher in the Rye.

By 4.30pm they were joined outside the building by
three other fans, including Paul Goresh who was an
amateur photographer who often visited the Dakota. Mark
struck up a conversation with Goresh and he proudly
showed Mark the album he had brought Lennon to sign.

Then, suddenly without any warning, Mark stood in
front of the man who had been his idol for so many
years. Mark was face-to-face with his obsession. He had
thought about John Lennon every day for more weeks
than he could remember. Now he was standing beside
him. John was walking out of the Dakota to a waiting
limousine with Yoko and a group of employees. Murder
was the last thing on Mark's mind. He was tongue-tied
and star struck as one of the world's greatest musicians,
and the object of so many of his thoughts, walked towards
him. John Lennon, radical leader of sixties youth culture,
outspoken hero of the working classes – there in the flesh
– ultra cool, relaxed, walking towards him. Speechless
Mark held the copy of *Double Fantasy* out in front of its
creator. Lennon took the pen and signed 'John Lennon,
December 1980' across the front.

In an interview with Adrian Wecer at Fishkill Prison
in 1981, Mark remembered their conversation:

He said "sure" and wrote his name, and when
he handed it back to me he looked at me and
kind of nodded his head, "Is that all you
want?". Like – just like that, like an enquiry
into a different matter, and I said "yeah, thanks

John". And he said again, "is that all you want…" and he asked twice, and I said, "yeah, thanks, that's all", or something like that. He got into the car and drove away.

Other unconfirmed reports suggest that Chapman confronted Lennon just before he got into his car with the possibility of joining his staff and that Lennon told him to send in his résumé. What is definite, however, is that the meeting happened. Paul Goresh was waiting with his camera and snapped one of the most haunting images a camera is ever likely to capture – John Lennon busily signing his name as his soon to be killer stood grinning beside him.

Mark's mind was awash with confusion. John Lennon had overwhelmed him with his sincerity and generosity. If the informal job application was true then Mark may have really believed that he could work for John and get even closer to the target. But why not kill him there and then? According to Chapman he was awestruck and knew that it was just not the right time to complete his 'mission'.

Mark offered Goresh $50 for the photograph. It was growing dark and by eight o'clock most observers had drifted away from the Dakota. Of the hardcore fans only Paul Goresh and Mark remained. Mark tried to persuade Paul to stay but Goresh knew that Lennon and the entourage were in the recording studio and it would be hours before they returned. He left shortly after eight, with the promise that he would return the next day with the photograph.

For the next three hours Mark shuffled around outside the Dakota, reading *The Catcher in the Rye* and every now and again talking to the doorman, Jose Perdomo. At 10:50pm a limousine pulled up. Yoko got out first. Then

Mark saw John. This was the moment – inside him the forces of good and evil, God and the Devil, were fighting for the upper hand. Lennon was approaching the door of the Dakota. He passed by Mark – too late Mark had missed his opportunity. Then a greater force overtook Mark Chapman. In a statement he made to the NYPD after his arrest Chapman said,

> He walked past me and then I heard in my head… do it, do it, do it, over and over again …

Just as John Lennon was about to reach the relative safety of the door of the Dakota, Mark called out, 'Mr Lennon'. As Lennon turned around Mark, crouched in his combat stance, took aim with his .38 revolver. As John turned again and tried to escape, Mark pulled the trigger. He emptied four of the five hollow point rounds into John Lennon. John didn't collapse immediately but managed to stagger forward about six paces before he fell, dying, beside the security hut at the entrance.

The Dakota concierge Jose Perdomo knocked the gun from Mark's hand and kicked it away. He screamed, 'Do you know what you've done?'. Mark seemed oblivious. He removed his hat and coat – he later told the police that he knew they were coming and he wanted them to see that he wasn't hiding a gun. Instead of running away he just stood on the sidewalk, pacing, reading *The Catcher in the Rye*.

The police were on the scene in minutes. Perdomo pointed out Chapman and they searched and handcuffed him before taking him away. Word spread quickly. Within an hour a crowd had gathered outside the Dakota. By 1am the crowd had swelled to an estimated 1,000 mourners. The vigil included aging hippies, some holding candles, some with photographs of the dead Lennon. Lennon's body had been taken to St Lukes-Roosevelt Hospital, and another crowd gathered there. Yoko asked doctors to delay the announcement of John's death. She said she didn't want Sean to hear it on the radio before she had the opportunity to tell him. (What a five year-old child would be doing listening to the radio at two in the morning is anyone's guess.)

Electronically, the word spread even quicker. In Los Angeles Lennon's death had occurred during the West Coast rush hour. By eight o'clock over 2,000 people had gathered for a candlelight vigil at Century City. People gathered across the country, from Washington DC to Washington State. The aftermath was a time of mourning and remembrance for the family and fans of John Lennon. The public revulsion at his death was compared to the feelings aroused by John F Kennedy's assassination, seventeen years previously. To Lennon's legions of adoring fans he was worshiped as a prince or emperor – his music and lyrics were treated as gospel. In Utah a thirty-year old man committed suicide, leaving a note saying that Lennon's death had taken away his will to live.

Lennon's assassination, almost instantaneously, rehabilitated his widow in the eyes of the world. Once seen as a controlling newcomer, who had taken John away from his fans, Yoko was now pitied and admired. No longer seen as an interfering freak, she was now seen as 'serene' and 'dignified' in her grief. Twenty-four hours after the murder she called for a 'time of silence' in John's memory. The tribute, scheduled for 2pm GMT on December 14, the Sunday following the murder, was widely observed. Black banner headlines filled the morning newspapers. Radio stations all over the globe observed the silence. Thousands gathered in cities from Sydney to

Paris, peaceful and respectful for the most part. New York City attracted the biggest number – 100,000 mourners gathered in Central Park, their emotions a combination of grief and shame. For New Yorkers there was an overwhelming feeling that John Lennon had made his home in their city and then had been murdered there. In Manhattan the flags flew at half-mast at the insistence of Mayor Ed Koch. All over the world people mourned the passing of a genius of his generation.

Mark Chapman had ensured that he would be famous forever. Possibly a significant part of what he had in mind all along, even back in his YMCA camp leaders days. He was now the centre of attention and relished the spotlight. Under questioning at the local precinct it became immediately apparent to police that they weren't dealing with an opportunist gunman. Chapman remained calm and composed throughout. His first statement to the police was factual but contained a reference to his alter ego:

> This morning I went to the bookstore and bought *The Catcher in the Rye*. I'm sure the large part of me is Holden Caulfield…. The small part of me must be the Devil. I went to the building. It's called the Dakota. I stayed there until he came out and asked him to sign my album. At that point my big part won and I wanted to go back to my hotel, but I couldn't. I waited until he came back …
>
> He came in a car. Yoko walked past first and I said hello, I didn't want to hurt her. Then John came and looked at me. I took the gun from my coat pocket and fired at him. I can't believe I could do that. I just stood there clutching the book. I didn't want to run away.

I don't know what happened to the gun. I
remember Jose kicking it away. Jose was crying
and telling me to please leave. I felt so sorry
for Jose. Then the police came and told me to
put my hands on the wall and cuffed me.'

By 1am his statement to police had expanded:

'...and I will not appeal any decision you have.
If it's a decision to keep me here in the prison,
I will not appeal it, and I never will. I'd like
the opportunity to apologize to Mrs. Lennon...'

And there's something else I want to say. I
feel that I see John Lennon now not as a
celebrity. I did then. I saw him as a cardboard
cutout on an album cover. I was very young
and stupid, and you get caught up in the media
and the records and the music. And now I –
I've come to grips with the fact that John
Lennon was a person. This has nothing to do
with being a Beatle or a celebrity or famous.
He was breathing, and I knocked him right
off his feet, and I don't feel because of that I
have any right to be standing on my feet here,
you know, asking for anything. I don't have a
leg to stand on because I took his right out
from under him, and he bled to death. And
I'm sorry that ever occurred.'

Chapman was charged with second-degree murder
and was taken to Bellevue Hospital, for psychiatric
examination. By now the public mood against Chapman
was turning ugly and there were a number of death threats
made against him. At Bellevue the windows were painted

black, after one caller said that Mark would be shot dead
by a sniper. He was then transferred to the relative safety
of Rikers Island prison. He was subjected to further
examination by a team of psychiatrists anxious to ascertain
if he could stand trial. During his tests he described his
relationship with Holden Caulfield and 'the little people'
in his head. He talked about all the people, besides Lennon,
who had crossed his mind as murder targets. Despite his
ramblings the doctors concluded that, while delusional,
he was competent to stand trial.

In January 1981, Chapman told psychologist Milton
Kline that he would use the trial to promote *The Catcher
in the Rye*.

> Everybody's going to be reading this book –
> with the help of the God-almighty media. ...
> They'll have to come out with a deluxe edition!

Out of the blue he announced to his legal team that he
planned to plead guilty as charged. They had been
preparing a defence case based on a plea of not guilty on
the grounds of diminished responsibility. He said that it
was an intervention from God. In court when Mark was
asked if he was guilty he replied: Yes, your honor, this is
my decision and God's decision. The judge accepted the
plea of guilty to second-degree murder. On August 24,
1981 he sentenced Chapman to a term of from twenty
years to life imprisonment. He also stipulated that
Chapman would not be eligible for parole until the turn
of the century.

Mark is now a prisoner in the famous Attica
Correctional Institution in New York State. By all accounts
Mark Chapman is a model prisoner. In his time at Attica
he has managed to keep clear of trouble and has even left

his delusions behind. Gloria flies in from Hawaii to visit him every three months or so. He still remains one of the most notorious prisoners in the American correctional system, receiving hundreds of letters every year.

Chapman's first parole hearing in 2000 led to thousands of activists organising a worldwide petition against his release, mainly though the Internet. His most recent parole hearing, in Autumn 2002, again denied him freedom. The Board said that releasing Mark David Chapman would '... deprecate the seriousness of the crime'. Stating that he had behaved in an 'acceptable' way in prison, they went on to say that this didn't guarantee that Mark Chapman wouldn't pose a threat to society.

The worldwide shock that followed John Lennon's assassination in many ways obscured the fact that his murder was the first notable case of celebrity stalking. The stalking, and in some cases assassination, of senior political figures had become an occupational hazard since the murder of President Abraham Lincoln in 1865. Lennon's murder highlighted, for the first time, that celebrities were subject to a similar occupational hazard. It was now evident that with celebrity status and influence came a certain degree of risk. Lennon's assassination demonstrated that when fan worship became obsession, the line between adoration and hatred became dangerously thin.

In Mark Chapman's deluded mental state he believed that his relationship with John Lennon was very special. At one point he would have done anything for Lennon. What drove Chapman over the edge was his belief that Lennon, his idol, had irrevocably betrayed him. This, combined with a deeply delusional mental state and a range of outside forces such as his alter-ego relationship with JD Salinger's Holden Caulfield, led him to the Dakota building on December 8, 1980. When Mark Chapman pulled the trigger the phenomenon of celebrity stalking was born.

CHAPTER TWO

I'm Your Biggest Fan

Love Obsession is a condition where a stalker almost always does not know his or her victim except through the media. According to Zona, Sharma and Lane, many in this group '...hold the delusion that they are loved by their victim'. In most cases the obsession is restricted to no more than an acute case of fan worship; But when fan worship becomes delusional fixation the potential for tragedy is enormous.

Movie directors are not always celebrities, with their own fan base. They certainly earn the same as the stars and appear to live the same jet-set lifestyles but they don't usually have the same level of appeal. However, increasingly as with football managers, some movie directors are now classified in the same star grouping as the actors or footballers themselves. They command the same respect and offer the same level of appeal. Nine out of ten people asked the question: 'Who is the world's most famous living film director?', will invariably answer with the same name – Steven Spielberg. The Ohio born, son of Jewish immigrants, is undoubtedly one of the most successful, prolific and pioneering directors of the modern age. The majority of movie directors live through the images and stories they create. They let the actors do the talking for them and, in many cases, accept most of the credit. Spielberg is one of the few exceptions to this rule.

Born on December 18, 1946, in Cincinnati, Steven Spielberg was the first-born, only boy of four children. His father, Arnold Spielberg, was an electrical engineer, involved in the early development of computers. His mother, Leah Adler, is a former concert pianist. As a child Steven watched a lot of television. Influenced by this fledgling entertainment vehicle and an early introduction to movies, he began to use his father's 8mm camera to shoot his own short movies.

In 1954 the family moved to Arizona where Arnold had found a new job. They moved into a house in Scottsdale, a middle-class area that was no more than a suburb of Phoenix in those days. The move had the effect of disengaging Spielberg from his earliest friends who he left behind in the mid-west. He had to make a new start in Arizona.

Spielberg went to Scottsdale's Arcadia High School where he avoided academia and sport but became a member of the Boy Scouts, began to study the clarinet and marched in the school band. In an effort to make new friends Steven started holding puppet shows. As he became a teenager, two major influences began to dominate Spielberg's life – movies and Judaism.

In 1959, in accordance with Jewish tradition, the thirteen-year old Spielberg celebrated his Bar Mitzvah. The ceremony, with its accompanying rituals, is an acknowledgment that a boy has completed the journey to manhood and is now ready to take his place among the adults of the world. To participate in the Bar Mitzvah ceremony Steven had to study Jewish history and law, particularly the aspects relating to Jewish persecution, most notably the Holocaust. This study provided Steven with a deep-rooted sense of his Jewish identity and an inspiration for later work. Nowhere is Steven Spielberg's Jewish commitment more publicly demonstrated than on the walls of the Holocaust Museum in Washington DC. The building, which houses a number of exhibitions about the 'Shoah', as it is known in Hebrew, was supported largely through public donations and foundation gifts from wealthy Jewish families. Four large marble tablets, over twenty feet each in height, dominate the entrance hall. On three of the tablets are inscribed the tightly packed names of many of the donor families. The minimum donation was believed to be $250,000. The fourth tablet stands out in stark contrast to the others. It reads 'For my parents – Steven Spielberg'. One can only imagine the scale of the donation made to ensure the simplicity of that message.

Success as a film director came early. At twelve years of age, Spielberg made his first film with a script and actors and by age thirteen, he had won a contest with his forty-minute film *Escape to Nowhere*. In 1963 he made his first feature film, a science fiction short called *Firelight*. Every spare moment he had outside of school was spent working on the film. Nothing interrupted his focus. He got help from his local college with the sound and the school band recorded the soundtrack. The ultimate achievement was when *Firelight* was screened at Steven's local cinema.

When Steven was sixteen, his father moved the family again. This time he went to work for IBM in Saratoga, near San Francisco, California. Around the same time his parents separated. That same year, Steven went to Los Angeles to visit his uncle. The main attraction was always going to be a visit to one or more of the Hollywood studios. Spielberg spent much of his time that summer pestering his uncle to take him on studio visits. He even took a bus tour of the homes of the stars. For the young Spielberg, the studios were places of mystery excitement, adventure and promise.

After that summer, he returned to Saratoga and High School. In the following years, he would visit Los Angeles whenever he could, trying to get someone to look at his growing catalogue of films. Unsurprisingly, he was rejected at every turn.

Throughout High School he concentrated all of his non-academic efforts on making films. In California in the late 1960s the atmosphere was conducive towards the development of all Art forms. Amateur film-making fell firmly into that category and was encouraged by teachers and other enthusiasts; Many became involved in 'co-productions' with the budding director Steven Spielberg.

Film schools were very much in their infancy at that time and the options to pursue any full-time courses in the area were limited. Steven chose to go to California State University to study English, graduating with a Bachelor of Arts degree in 1970. More importantly however, by the time he finished university he had almost eight amateur film works to his credit.

His first real break came when his short film *Amblin* won an award at the Atlanta Film Festival. The publicity this generated culminated in Universal Studios offering Spielberg a job as a television director. The 1960's television boom had led a number of the big studios to diversify into the small screen. By this stage, Universal Studios had a long list of successful television products. Spielberg jumped at the opportunity to get behind the camera. His first notable success was directing the legendary Joan Crawford in the television movie *Night Gallery*. He also directed episodes of two of the most popular television drama hits of the 1970s – *Columbo* and

Marcus Welby, MD. He also made some movies, one of which, *Duel*, was a critical success and was released in cinemas around Europe.

The Sugarland Express, released in 1974, was his first big screen feature film for Universal. The film was generally considered to be a credible début but it was only a mediocre box office success. Luckily by then Spielberg had acquired the rights to Peter Benchley's best-selling book, *Jaws* and was all set to direct the film.

The production of *Jaws* was so difficult Spielberg was almost replaced as director. There were problems with the budget, the weather, the special effects and the crew. Despite these enormous obstacles *Jaws* won three Academy Awards, including Best Picture, and became one of the biggest box office hits of all time. Spielberg was catapulted into the major league of movie making and became a Hollywood hot property overnight.

For his next landmark project *Close Encounters of the Third Kind* in 1977, he joined forces with his friend George Lucas. The Lucas/Spielberg relationship developed over the years as the two teamed up to make the extremely popular *Indiana Jones* trilogy. Spielberg's reputation and fame continued to grow. In 1982 he produced and directed *ET*. The film was critically acclaimed, won a number of Oscars and immediately broke box office records.

Meanwhile Spielberg's personal life was also changing. In 1979, he met the actress Amy Irwing. They were married shortly afterwards. The Spielbergs were now part of Hollywood royalty. With Hollywood celebrity come the trappings of that exalted status. Spielberg was, for the first time, constantly being recognised in the street. He was also offered better tables in restaurants and special attention at VIP events. He began to receive fan mail and, inevitably, pester or hate letters. For every ten people who wrote telling him that they loved him or his work, there was always one who sent hate mail or a begging letter. The need to protect his privacy was becoming more intense by the movie and, for the first time, Spielberg retained security personnel at his home and on his location shoots.

In 1984 his personal life took a new turn. While auditioning actresses for *Indiana Jones and the Temple of Doom* he met Kate Capshaw. She went on to star in the film along side Harrison Ford. Kate was married to Robert Capshaw and they had one daughter. The attraction between Capshaw and Spielberg was instantaneous and their subsequent relationship the catalyst for their mutual divorces. Spielberg divorced Amy in 1989 and two years later he married the newly-divorced Kate. She converted to Judaism before the wedding, confirming Spielberg's deep commitment to his religion and their joint commitment to the relationship.

Spielberg kick-started the nineties with two monster hits. *Jurassic Park* set new attendance records and was thought to be the best special effects film ever. *Schlinder's List* was a movie that had been in the planning stages for over ten years. Based on Thomas Keneally's award-wining book, *Schindler's Ark*, it tells the tale of Oskar Schindler, a Nazi who risked his life and fortune to save Jews from the gas chambers. Three hours long and shot in black and white the film was a box office giant. Spielberg won his first Oscar for Best Director.

In 1994 Spielberg achieved a long-standing ambition when he formed Dreamworks SKG with David Geffen and Jeffrey Katzenberg. Established to rival the major studios, the company reaffirmed Spielberg's position as one of the most powerful figures in Hollywood.

By the mid-1990s Steven Spielberg was at the height

of his profession. His family life had also expanded. Kate and Steven's family now included Max (his son with his former wife Amy); Sasha, Sawyer, adopted daughters Theo and Mikhela, step-daughter Jessica, and Destry-Allyn. The couple had moved to a new home at Amalfi Drive, in the affluent Pacific Palisades suburb of Los Angeles. The house is set on a pretty avenue lined with foliage of all kinds. The high walls and daunting security gates give nothing away about the scale of the house, which lies behind them. This is one of the most exclusive areas of suburban Los Angeles and security devices, such as closed circuit cameras and foot patrols, are everywhere. The couple and their children maintained a low-key existence and very few people recognised the Spielbergs as they went about their daily business. To those who did notice them, the discreet nature of their personal security arrangements meant that the family appeared perfectly normal. Anyone who tried to enter the family's property was politely, but firmly, moved on. Steven Spielberg may have become America's favourite director but he knew the dangers associated with his sort of celebrity. He made sure that neither himself nor his family would be an easy target for potential stalkers.

By 1997, Spielberg was ready to embark on his most ambitious project yet. *Saving Private Ryan* tells the story of a group of eight soldiers sent to find the last surviving of four sons from the one family sent to Europe during World War II. Starring Tom Hanks and Matt Damon, the movie would go on to take $460 million at the box office.

On June 20, 1997 the Spielbergs departed for Ireland. They were shooting the D-Day landing scenes on location at Curracloe beach in County Wexford, on Ireland's south-east coast. Their house at 1515 Amalfi Drive would be empty for most of the summer but an overt security presence was maintained around the clock. This is fairly common practice among the rich and famous of Hollywood. In addition to the organised bus tours of the stars' homes there are plenty of informal visitors to Hollywood homes who hope to catch a glimpse of their heroes and to see their houses. Some fans even try to have a look around the gardens or try to get even closer.

Stephen Lopez was stationed at 1515 Amalfi Drive to ensure that they didn't get too close. Lopez was a police officer with the Los Angeles Police Department (LAPD), assigned to the organized crime and vice division. In common with many of his colleagues, he also worked part-time for the Berman & Ely company, providing home security and protection for the more affluent residents of Los Angeles, including Steven Spielberg and his family. They screened all incoming packages and also people trying to get onto the property. Lopez had been working for Spielberg for about ten years.

On June 29 he was working an evening shift at the house. He was in plainclothes and was armed. Just before six o'clock Lopez noticed somebody in a white jeep pull up to the gate. Lopez thought this a little unusual. It was normal for tourists to buy one of the 'stars' homes maps' and identify the Spielberg house, which was featured on most of them. Generally though the tourists would drive by slowly and stare in to try and see what they could. Occasionally a tourist might get out and take a photo of the house through the gates; The odd one might even ask to speak to Spielberg or try to leave a script for him. But this individual did not do any of those things.

The man drove onto the driveway and got out of the car. He approached the black communications box where he could talk to the security office via the intercom. The driver said he was there to see 'Mr Spielberg'. Lopez knew no visitors were expected because the security team had been given a list of callers. Anyway, Spielberg was in Ireland. The request, although not unusual for a tourist, put Lopez on his guard. The man identified himself as Jonathan Norman and said that he worked for Mr Geffen. He asked Lopez if he could '...go to his [Spielberg's] house and knock on his door and ask to speak to him?' When Lopez asked him to leave Norman seemed confused. The detective stood his ground until Norman realised that he wasn't going to get in and drove away. In the ten years he had worked at the Spielberg residence, Lopez had never encountered an incident similar to this one. Although Lopez didn't log information on everybody who visited the house he logged Norman's details. He thought this visitor was different.

Jonathan Norman hadn't been considered in any way different for most of his life. In fact he started life as the epitome of the regular All-American kid. Born in Salt Lake City, Utah in 1967, Jonathan and his family were as reserved and conservative as most families in that most conservative of US States. The family was affluent and money was never a problem. Jonathan was a model child, a good sportsman and an attentive and diligent student. In fact all appeared normal until his father just 'took off' one day. His mother, later described by Norman's Public Defender John Lawson as 'a level headed woman', tried hard to keep her family together after Jonathan's father effectively left them to fend for themselves. His father's busy lifestyle and ultimate departure bred a huge resentment in his son. According to Lawson:

'... his father just wasn't there for him. Because
he did a lot of travelling and was almost never

at home, he instilled in Jonathan a desperate
need for a father figure.'

One particular incident that later came to light,
demonstrates the behavioural difficulties Jonathan started
to have because of his family problems. He drove to a
Seven Eleven store in Salt Lake with a friend. They were
driving away from the store when Jonathan suddenly
spotted a man sitting outside it and stopped the car. He
jumped out and, without any exchange taking place or
any apparent provocation, attacked the man and started
beating him up. This incident occurred at around the
same time that the family was going through its roughest
patch.

As soon as he was old enough, Jonathan went to
California to escape the claustrophobic surroundings of
Salt Lake and his unhappy home life. He was extremely
interested in the entertainment industry and wanted to
become an actor. Hollywood was the place to be. It was
also a city where he could explore his developing bisexual
tendencies more openly and freely. He worked, as most
aspiring actors do, in a variety of low-paid, dead-end jobs
to supplement whatever acting work he could get. He
also worked on developing his body and for a time was a
permanent fixture at his local gym, developing a muscular
physique, partly to keep in shape for whatever film
opportunities might come his way and partly to maintain
the muscular body favoured by some gay men. He worked
mainly in construction where his physical strength was
an attribute and, for quite some time, as an assistant in a
casting and management agency. He felt that working in
an agency meant that he was still close to the film industry
and that he would get a first look at the parts that came
in. But this strategy didn't seem to work out. His acting

efforts came to almost nothing; Making a commercial seems to be all the acting work he ever got and was his highest achievement as an actor.

Norman drifted from job to job for a while and became involved in drugs, particularly methamphetamine. At this point, Jonathan's life didn't seem to have any direction. His career as an actor had largely failed. On an emotional level, he still felt a great deal of resentment towards his father for abandoning him, a state of mind possibly exacerbated by his use of drugs. It is also possible that it was at this time that he targeted Steven Spielberg and became obsessed with meeting him because he became fixated on the idea of finding a father. In Norman's mind the two men had much in common. He seemed to have viewed Spielberg as a surrogate father. In Utah, Norman's father had been an important figure. He was deeply involved in politics and was involved in powerful financial deals. In terms of Hollywood and on a bigger world scale, Norman saw Spielberg in the same light. Dreamworks SKG and most especially its main movers, Spielberg, Katzenberg and Geffen, were hugely powerful figures in Hollywood. In Norman's confused mind, Spielberg made a very attractive father-figure.

Jonathan Norman's visit on June 29 was only the beginning of his stalking campaign against Steven Spielberg. Nancy and Perry Altshule also live on Amalfi Drive, about a block away from the Spielberg residence. Early on the morning of July 11 Nancy awoke to hear a woman shouting, 'Get out of my yard'. Through a haze of sleep, Nancy figured that their swimming pool repairman had gone next door by mistake. Looking out the window she noticed the man was now in her garden and went out to investigate. She quickly realised that he had nothing to do with her swimming pool. He was standing outside on the patio holding a curtain rod over his head like a javelin. Nancy recalls, 'He looked at me and he said, get out of here.' She was petrified and ran back into the house and called the police on 911 as she watched him go around the side of her house.

As 911 just kept ringing out Nancy called Westec. Westec is a private security firm which operates a rapid response service in the Pacific Palisades area of Los Angeles. She also rang her sister-in-law who lives nearby. Nancy told her there was a crazy guy in the area and to lock her doors. The 'crazy guy', it would subsequently transpire, was Jonathan Norman.

At around 7am, Westec security officer Manual Hernandez answered a call from a woman who had seen someone in her backyard. She told Hernandez that the man had been walking back and forth flapping his arms. He had then left her yard through the back fence and had gone on to somebody else's property. Hernandez had just started checking the property for damage when he received a similar call from a house about a block and a half away. The man fitted the same description. Hernandez quickly responded and arrived just in time to see a man coming out of some bushes. The man ran across the garden, through the side gate and jumped through the back gate. Hernandez saw a large stick in his right hand. As he walked towards the house, Nancy met him and told him the man had to be on the street somewhere. Hernandez called for back-up.

When back-up arrived the group of officers followed the trail. They looked into a house, which was the back end house on Amalfi Drive. The owners told them that they had found a man in their backyard who had run off when questioned. They came to an address about two and a half blocks from Spielberg's house. The man had entered a house he knew was empty, as it was under construction. They found Norman hiding in the backyard. When he saw the officers outside, he ran off again. Hernandez eventually found him hiding in some bushes. Norman raised his hands and something, which looked like a book, dropped from them. They did a quick body search for weapons and led him out of the property. The local police weren't far behind and Norman was handed over to the LAPD.

Hernandez picked-up the black book Norman had dropped and gave it to the arresting officers. It contained pictures and cutouts from a newspaper. Hernandez later recalled Norman saying that he was Steven Spielberg's adopted son. He said that he had just been adopted the day before and that the jackal was trying to get him, which is why he was running away from everybody. Hernandez thought that he was high on drugs of some sort.

The LAPD had received a 415 call, indicating that someone was causing a disturbance, at about the same time Manuel Hernandez was responding to his second call. When they arrived on the scene the Westec officers already had Norman in custody. Officer Linda Peace remembers the diary. It was full of pictures of Spielberg and an actress. She also remembers Norman saying he was Spielberg's adopted son and that he went by the name of Jonathan or David Spielberg or Jonathan David Spielberg. Peace thought the man was extremely weird.

Norman was detained at West LA station. His behaviour was so strange that Linda Peace suggested he be examined by one of her colleagues, Donald Goosens, a police officer working undercover with the LAPD narcotics division. Goosens has received detailed training and is experienced in the area of investigating people under the influence of certain drugs. He examined Jonathan Norman at around 11 o'clock that morning. Before the examination he could hear the man in the background talking incoherently. Goosens first checked him for phencyclidine or PCP, a methamphetamine drug, which can have many psychological effects. PCP makes the body temperature rise and the body reeks from the smell of ether, which is the primary ingredient of PCP. Norman did not have this smell, there was no abnormal heat coming from his skin and his pupils didn't have nystagmus, a bouncing of the eyes, which is another symptom of PCP use. The drug methamphetamine also causes the pupils to become very large and the user to speak very rapidly. It leads to a very high pulse rate. When Goosens examined Norman, everything was within the average range. His pulse rate was 72 and his pupils were normal. As far as Goosens was concerned, Norman had not taken methamphetamine.

Later that morning Norman was released without charge. The police felt at this point that, despite Goosens' analysis, Norman was not fully in possession of his senses. While he had trespassed on property, they put his weird manner down to some sort of unusual, and probably temporary, mental state. He hadn't really been threatening in his behaviour but seemed more odd than sinister at that point. Rather than detain him, he was released with a warning. But the warning wasn't enough to deter him from his mission.

By five o'clock that evening, Norman was back on Amalfi Drive. Steve Lopez had just finished his shift and was being relieved by another off-duty police officer, Lou Kovin. The two men were chatting together in the security office. As Steve Lopez walked out the gate he noticed a dark blue *Land Rover* parked directly behind his own car. This struck him as odd because there was plenty of parking on the street. It was so close that Lopez was worried that his car might be damaged. He routinely noticed that its license plate was 3 SNJ 537. Lopez walked over and checked out his car. Then he realised that there was a man sitting in the driver's seat of the *Land Rover*. The man was trying to hide, so Lopez stood and watched his movements.

Steve stood there silently for a while and as he walked away he realised that the man in the car was Jonathan Norman. He remembered Norman's previous attempt to get into the property to see Spielberg. Now he was parked behind Steve's car trying to hide. Lopez felt that the only reason for this behaviour was that Norman was checking out the security on the house and trying to determine what time the shifts changed. Getting into his car, he called Lou Kovin and told him to call the police immediately. Then he drove back into the Spielberg property. The Spielberg house is on about five acres, and has a six-foot high fence all around the perimetre. The only way Lopez and Kovin could watch the *Land Rover* was on the security cameras. They zoomed in on the front windshield so they could see him clearly. Every time a car drove by he would pick up some papers or something to try and cover his face.

Suddenly, the engine on the *Land Rover* was started and Norman prepared to leave. But he did something odd first. He drove up the road and backed his car into the northern driveway of the house. Then he kept the car in reverse and began banging repeatedly against the gates. The guards felt that Norman was trying to see how much force was needed to open them. Lopez recalls that over the years he had seen people do U-turns and other unusual manoeuvres, but nobody had ever come that close to the gates uninvited. After about a minute, Norman drove off northbound on Amalfi Drive.

Officer Scott Burkett and his partner, Officer Sandra Donaway, had received a 415 on a male suspect at about 6pm. The man, a possible prowler, was in the Amalfi Drive area. They recognised Steven Spielberg's address and sped over. Steve Lopez quickly told them about what he had just witnessed and that he'd noted the same man behaving very strangely around the compound of the house about two weeks previously. There was now no sign of Norman, but he hadn't travelled very far. Lopez, with the police officers, soon found the blue *Land Rover* a short distance away but there was no sign of the prowler. Lopez returned to the house while the police officers continued on their routine patrol.

Within minutes the officers passed the *Land Rover* again and this time Burkett noticed a man at the passenger's side of the vehicle with the door open. He didn't know what the man was doing but he matched the description. Approaching the car cautiously, they established that the man was Jonathan Norman. They ordered him to step out of the car, asking him to place his hands on his head as he did so. After searching him Burkett quickly handcuffed him. He then noticed a bulky package on his waistband. Tentatively unwrapping it he found, to his surprise, some duct tape and handcuffs. Realising that they had discovered something far beyond their initial expectations, they began a further body search. It revealed a box cutter knife blade and razor blades in his pockets. While Scott Burkett kept an eye on Norman, Sandra Donaway began to search the car. The first discovery was car rental papers in a briefcase along with a day planner. She also found two sets of handcuffs and a lot of papers with writing all over them. It was difficult to decipher all of the writing but most of the pages had one thing in common – Steven Spielberg's name featured on almost all of them. Donaway removed a lot of items from the car and, as Norman looked on, they began to sift their way through them. They immediately noticed some traffic tickets detailing the *Land Rover's* registration. They also found other traffic tickets against a white jeep.

As they worked on, removing more material from the car, the officers continued to question Norman about the reason for his behaviour and why he was hanging around Amalfi Drive. They had found out from their base that Norman had already been detained earlier that day for much the same reason. Answering with a degree of credibility that the officers found hard to disbelieve, Norman told them that he had an appointment with Spielberg and that he wanted to deliver a screenplay that he had prepared. It was important, he told them, that he showed it to the director in person. They asked him what the screenplay was about. He replied that it was '…about a man raping another man'. He said that the handcuffs and duct tape were props and that they were an important part of the movie he was hoping to make with Spielberg. Between coherent statements, Burkett remembered that Norman was murmuring and mumbling and rambling on. It was clear to both officers that Jonathan Norman was determined in his objective to meet Spielberg but delusional about the nature of his relationship with the director.

Norman was taken to West LA Police station, for the second time in twelve hours, where he was detained prior to being charged. The *Land Rover* was temporarily impounded and searched for more clues. Almost everything taken from it had something to do with Spielberg and Norman's supposed 'relationship' with him. The car was eventually returned to its owners, Enterprise

Rent-a-car and the branch manager, Ed Sosnoski, was interviewed.

Sosnoski remembered Norman changing to the *Land Rover* from a *Cherokee* jeep on July 8. As Steve Lopez had noted, Norman was driving the jeep when he first called to Spielberg's house on June 29. Jonathan Norman had first contacted sales representative Nicole Rashon Smith on June 25, when she rented him the *Cherokee* jeep. The next time she saw Norman was on July 8. He said he'd been having problems with the jeep and wanted a different car. He told her that he was unable to leave his home so she met him and they exchanged cars. As they were doing this she helped him move some of the items that he had in the jeep into the *Land Rover*. There were bags of clothes, a videotape of *ET* and some papers. Nicole remembered the mess the jeep was in but she also remembered the contents because of their connection with Spielberg.

When the police returned the *Land Rover* to Enterprise, the staff there found more evidence of Norman's obsession with Spielberg. Both Nicole and Ed Sosnoski noticed pictures and magazine cutouts of Spielberg in the back of the car. The *ET* video was still there, along with some bottles of what looked like medication of some sort. There was also a 35 millimetre camera, batteries, a watch, a scissors, a box of about fifty razor blades, sunglasses, a hat and an article about the movie *The Lost World*. The *Land Rover* also contained a lot of clothes and a laundry basket.

Norman was now in custody awaiting questioning. His bizarre claims of being related to Spielberg, along with his mumblings about rape, were enough to make police believe that he was a potential danger. The information about his repeated visits to the Spielberg

residence and the unusual items found in his possession
at his arrest compounded this view. Given his mental
condition Norman was referred for psychiatric evaluation
to Harbor-UCLA Medical Center. The hospital is located
in Torrance in the southwestern coastal region of Los
Angeles County.

In Steven Spielberg's absence, the LAPD police had
been talking to his closest legal advisor. Bruce Ramer has
been Steven Spielberg's lawyer for over twenty-five years.
The security men at Amalfi Drive had also filled Ramer
in on the day's events. They also told Ramer how Jonathan
Norman had first tried to get on to the Spielberg property
two weeks earlier claiming that he worked for David
Geffen. The security men also told him about the first
incident that morning and the subsequent incident that
same evening. Bruce Ramer found Norman's claims that
his name was David Spielberg and that Spielberg had
adopted him particularly worrying. But worse was to
follow. The LAPD told Ramer that in an interview
Norman had revealed that it was his intention to rape
Steven Spielberg.

Bruce Ramer then faced a dilemma – an awkward task
had just been forced upon him. He was uneasy about
telling Steven about the intended rape. It was not the
kind of information he felt comfortable telling anyone, let
alone a client and friend. Added to this, Spielberg was in
the middle of directing a film and was obviously going to
be focused on that. However, Jonathan Norman had
already made three attempts to reach Spielberg. In case
there was any chance of a fourth attempt, Steven had to
be made aware that he had become the target of a
potentially dangerous stalker.

Ramer contacted Steven in Ireland and passed on all
the information he had about Jonathan Norman.

Spielberg's immediate reaction was complete disbelief. He was used to fans asking for autographs and sending him scripts but nothing like this had ever happened to him before. He did not know Jonathan Norman and was certainly not related to him. Ramer then told him about the items that they had found in the car including the handcuffs, the duct tape and the razor knife. He also told him that in subsequent interviews Norman had stated that he was there to do Spielberg harm.

Spielberg became completely panicked and upset as Ramer gave him more details. Ramer told him about Norman's state of mind and clearly thought that he was a very realistic threat to Spielberg and his family. Spielberg was afraid to tell his wife for fear of upsetting her. He kept the details of the call to himself. From Ramer's account, Spielberg believed that Norman was on a dangerous 'mission', and that if he had not been caught, he would have completed this "mission'. Spielberg was later to say that he truly felt his life was in danger.

Spielberg was told about the information contained in the notebooks found in the *Land Rover*. Norman had amassed a dossier on Spielberg, his family, all the key people at Dreamworks and details of his other studio office at Amblin Entertainment. There were details about his sisters, his wife and even minute details about his own age and height. But what particularly upset Spielberg was the information about his children, which Norman had amassed in precise detail. Spielberg knew that in Los Angeles, and in particular in the Hollywood area, it wasn't unusual for people to be observant, and to watch and learn things about famous people. However knowing that Norman's underlying intention, while amassing so much information, was to injure or even kill, absolutely chilled him.

From his location in Ireland he immediately feared for his mother, Leah Adler, whom he felt was very vulnerable. She had lived alone on Wilshire Boulevard since his stepfather had died. She was still in Los Angeles that summer while Spielberg and his family were abroad. Spielberg told his mother what was happening and provided security for her immediately. He also upgraded the security around his family. He already had some in place for his stays in Ireland and London, but now he insisted that his children were accompanied at all times, even when they were just sightseeing.

The opening sequence in *Saving Private Ryan* features a twenty-five-minute scene from the 1944 invasion of Normandy, focusing on the first landings at Omaha Beach. The scenes featured hundreds of soldiers, mostly from the Irish Army. They were shooting from tanks, cannons and guns using blanks to recreate the atmosphere of the attacks. Spielberg later testified that he was terrified that Norman could have shown up in Ireland and put on an American army uniform and infiltrated the set without attracting undue attention. Spielberg believed it was possible that he could have accessed a real gun with live ammunition and caused a great deal of harm and even death. This possibility forced Spielberg to take this threat seriously, something that he had never had to do previously. He employed more off-duty officers to do extra work at the house on Amalfi Drive, in case Norman came back to harm the people that were living there in his absence and whom he considered part of the family.

For the immediate future, however, there was little chance of Norman doing anything. Police had begun to uncover more details about his unusual life and his bizarre 'mission' against the director. On July 21 Paul Wright interviewed Norman. Wright is a detective with the LAPD, and at that time he was assigned to the Threat Management Unit. This unit was established to investigate cases of stalking and excessive behaviour and to take action where appropriate. On Spielberg's instructions Bruce Ramer had engaged another law firm to file for a temporary restraining order against Norman, to prevent him from interfering, stalking or threatening Spielberg or his family. Initial complaints and legal filings by the Spielberg legal team indicated that the LAPD would be investigating, and potentially prosecuting, a case of stalking by Jonathan Norman – stalking is the special preserve of the Threat Management Unit.

Wright's interview with Norman took place at Los Angeles County Jail where Norman was now being held in custody. Norman told Wright that he would speak to him without an attorney. Wright wanted to find out why he had visited Spielberg's residence on the two occasions the police knew about. Norman told Wright that he had had an obsession for Spielberg for approximately a month. He described his obsession as a sexual one. Thinking of Spielberg and being with him caused him to 'jack off'. This then developed into an obsession where Norman felt he just had to be with Spielberg. Norman also told Wright that he believed Spielberg wanted to be raped by him and that was why he brought handcuffs and duct tape. He said that when he was outside the house at 1515 Amalfi Drive on July 11, he had been pacing about to determine how best to get into the property. He constantly thought about how best to carry out the rape. Norman said that he had tried to get through the gate of the compound on another occasion but had been stopped by security men. This was most likely June 29, the evening he had been confronted by Steve Lopez. Norman said he thought he had been over at Amalfi Drive on one other occasion but he couldn't remember for sure. Norman described what happened that morning. He said he was walking around and pacing the compound, checking distances. He had attempted to jump the fence to get into Spielberg's compound but had been chased off by a ferocious dog. His reason for doing all of this was that he intended get into the property to rape Steven Spielberg.

Norman claimed that he had taken a large amount of methamphetamine before the incident on July 11 and that taking the drugs had made him stay awake for three days. This admission didn't square up with Officer Goosens' examination when he'd determined that Norman hadn't taken the drug. It must be noted, however, that Goosens performed a straightforward observational examination and not an urinalysis, which would have put the issue beyond any doubt. A further test performed on Norman at the Harbor-UCLA Medical Center showed that he was 'presumptive positive' for amphetamines, meaning that there were traces of the drug in his system.

As the interview progressed Norman told Wright that he had learned all his detailed information about Spielberg through a variety of magazines, including *People* and *The Hollywood Reporter*. He said that it was no longer his intention to pursue Spielberg. He believed that the drugs he had taken were what induced him to do the things that he had done. As the investigating officer in the case, Wright was only too well aware of the items that had been recovered, such as the duct tape and the handcuffs. He had also studied Norman's day-planner and the notebooks, most especially details of Spielberg's life. Most worrying for the police, and damning from Norman's point of view, was a checklist of items needed to facilitate the crime he intended to commit. The documents contained a 'shopping list' which included the following items; 3 x eye masks, 3 x handcuffs, 4 x pairs of nipple clippers, 3 x dog collars, 3 x locks with the same key, 4 x packs of blades, chloroform and a shocker. Norman never said anything about hurting anyone but Spielberg. However Wright was troubled when he saw that the names of Spielberg's children were listed in the day planner. The spelling of some difficult names was correct down to the last letter. Wright felt that, in his professional opinion, this indicated that there was definitely a threat to the children.

As far as Wright is concerned Norman also demonstrated the sort of split personality disorder that he has seen in bisexual men over many years of policing in Los Angeles.

> 'These guys who are torn between homo and
> heterosexuality can often become very violent
> as a result of their internal sexual conflicts.'

Wright believed that a combination of rage at his father and a growing sexual confusion certainly contributed to Norman's condition.

Further confirmation of Norman's erratic and unpredictable behavioural patterns came from Charles 'Chuck' Markovich. Chuck Markovich had been a good friend of Jonathan's for over six years. Norman had lived with Markovich three times. Both men were openly homosexual but although they had an intimate friendship Chuck claimed they were never actually lovers. Norman contacted Chuck from Harbor-UCLA and persuaded him to go to Enterprise Rent-a-car and pick up some of the things he had left in the *Land Rover*. On July 18, a week after the incident at Amalfi Drive, Chuck also cleared out Norman's apartment. When police heard about the two incidents they decided to interview Chuck.

At the interview Markovich not only gave them details about Norman's lifestyle he was also able to fill in the days up to Norman's arrest. He told the investigators that thirty-year-old Jonathan was unemployed and that he had seen him use methamphetamine. He also told them that he believed Norman was a schizophrenic and claimed to have seen his medical records. Markovich said that Norman was totally paranoid. He would put sheets up over the windows and he always thought somebody was after him or watching him.

On Wednesday, July 9, 1997, Chuck and Jonathan had spent the evening at Markovich's apartment. Chuck remembered Norman suddenly announcing that there was a portion of Steven Spielberg's perimetre wall that was small enough for him to jump over. According to Chuck, Jonathan said he wanted to go over to Spielberg's house that night and rape him. Markovich already knew where Spielberg's house was because a week earlier Norman had taken him there. Markovich told Norman he was being ridiculous and pointed out that there were guards on duty and that he would never be able to get over the wall. Norman seemed to agree and the subject was dropped. Chuck believed Norman didn't go to Spielberg's house that night but he was very concerned about his state of mind. He thought he might actually try to jump the perimetre wall. Norman had already told him about another time when he had gone to Spielberg's house and the guards wouldn't let him in. It was clear to Chuck that Norman was not content with just stalking Spielberg from a distance. Chuck went on to tell the police that Jonathan had shown him some pictures from his day planner. He had pointed to one in particular which was a picture of a young man with a nice body. The man was naked and

Spielberg's face was pasted on top of his head.

Next morning, July 10, Jonathan called around to Chuck's apartment just as he was getting ready to leave for work. Norman had brought over a laundry basket full of dirty clothes to wash. Chuck asked him what he was doing. Norman said he wasn't sure exactly but that he needed to be out of his apartment by July 15, so he thought he would slowly move his stuff back into Markovich's place. This was something that they had not discussed and they had a fight about it – Norman stormed out of the apartment.

Markovich noticed he'd left his wallet behind and went after him. When he went out, he found that Norman's papers were scattered around the entrance to the apartment building. By now Norman had calmed down and Markovich gave him the wallet and went off to work.

The next time he saw Norman was the following Wednesday, July 14, at Harbor-UCLA Harbor Medical Center. The first thing he noticed was Norman's appearance. He looked rough, untidy and completely different. He usually wore pressed cotton shirts and was very neat. Norman told him that he was now going for the 'Rambo look'. It appears that Jonathan had remained dressed like this since the incidents at Amalfi Drive. He told Chuck all about what had happened at Spielberg's house.

On July 15, Jonathan Norman was released into Chuck's care. He said that he did not want Spielberg's name mentioned and if he brought it up, Markovich was to stop him. Chuck recalled that later that day they went to a movie. Norman wanted to see Spielberg's *The Lost World*. While they were watching the movie, he made some strange comments involving Spielberg. He mentioned that there was a mother and a father T-Rex and a baby and Spielberg was the father and David was the mother and

John was the baby. Chuck had no idea what Jonathan was talking about. He thought that as Jonathan had just spent some time in a psychiatric facility he couldn't be all that well mentally. However, he had taken special note of Jonathan's references to the family and to his father in particular.

It was only when police questioned Markovich that they were able to piece together the possible background that might explain Norman's obsessive interest in Steven Spielberg. Chuck later told investigators that Norman's father had left him when he was six years old and that Jonathan had never been able to deal with it. He had always resented the fact that his father was never there for him. Chuck also told the police that he thought that Jonathan's father was very anti-gay. Norman felt that since Steven Spielberg's business partner, David Geffen, is homosexual this was proof that Spielberg was open-minded about sexuality. Markovich also felt that Norman looked on Spielberg as a father figure. This is what he couldn't understand at all – why would Jonathan want to rape Spielberg if he saw him as the father he felt he never had?

Detectives got a search warrant for Chuck Markovich's apartment. Patrick McPherson, the chief investigator for the District Attorney's office served the warrant on August 4. They started to search Jonathan's personal belongings. McPherson found lots of papers containing Spielberg's name and a map labeled 'movie stars' homes'. He recovered a business card labelled 'Probe Inc. Spytech Agency – Investigations by guard and surveillance'. Writing on the back of the card suggested that Norman had been looking at a camera that could take long-range photographs. There was an Internet biography, featuring Spielberg, Jeffrey Katzenberg and David Geffen, and the Dreamworks

Board of Directors. Another computer printout from 1994, referred to Katzenberg, Spielberg and Geffen, saying they were '...tossing Hollywood into a 'tiz' with their merger'. He found a magazine about *The Lost World* and noticed that pieces had been cut out. There was a cover of the book *Spielberg, a biography* featuring Spielberg's photograph. He also discovered a blue binder which was basically a daily record of their activities. McPherson noted that the entries were consistent with someone obsessed with an individual and their movements. There were sexual connotations to a large amount of the entries. Markovich told McPherson that he had never seen Norman accessing information on the Internet. He also said that in all the time he had known Jonathan, he had never heard him talk about any obsession prior to the one he had had for Spielberg.

The public procedure to imprison Jonathan Norman began on October 8, 1997. The appearance of Norman before a Grand Jury in *People of the State of California (Plaintiff) versus Jonathan Norman (Defendant)*, was convened to consider whether or not to indict Norman on a charge of stalking in violation of Penal code section 646.9(A). In opening the proceedings, Rhonda Saunders, Deputy District Attorney of the County of Los Angeles, and one of the foremost and internationally respected authorities on stalking, defined stalkers as:

> 'Every person who willfully, maliciously and repeatedly follows or harasses another person.'

This would constitute a violation of penal code 646.9 (A), as would 'making a credible threat', particularly one which was 'intended to place the victim in reasonable fear for his safety or the safety of his immediate family'.

Saunders claimed that Jonathan Norman stalked Steven Spielberg under all of these definitions. The prosecution case, which took two days to outline, featured numerous witnesses, including Steve Lopez, Chuck Marcovich and the victim, Steven Spielberg.

Spielberg's evidence was calmly delivered but left no doubt that the director believed that Jonathan Norman posed a real and continuing threat to himself and his family. He described himself as being '…very distraught over the possibility that this man could come out of jail and go right back on the warpath again'. He went on to say:

> 'It is something that obsesses me, I think about this all the time, it's always on my mind.'

Norman, by refusing to be legally represented, contributed to his own demise. In her closing statement, Rhonda Saunders, clinical in her delivery and execution, detailed the facts of the case from start to finish, working her way through Jonathan Norman's activities in late June and early July 1997. She finally asked the members of the Grand Jury to consider Norman's courtship of Spielberg. As she put it:

> 'Was he courting Spielberg? Was he bringing him flowers, a card or candy? No, he was bringing him handcuffs and duct tape. That shows his state of mind – that to instill fear was a major part of his plan.'

In order to return the indictment and allow the case to proceed to a full trial, fourteen or more jurors had to agree. The actual number assenting wasn't revealed when

the jury returned from their deliberations but their decision
found in favour of the indictment. The judge then asked
Rhonda Saunders for a recommendation as to bail.
Requesting a bail of one million dollars, she noted that
Norman was already on parole for two counts of assault
with a deadly weapon and that he posed an '...extremely
dangerous threat to the victim and the victim's family'.
The two convictions stemmed from a 1995 motoring
incident during which Norman had tried to run down a
group of pedestrians while driving a car. The bail bond
was set at $1 million and the trial for February 19, 1998.

The trial was heard in front of a jury of five men and
seven women at the Santa Monica Superior Court. Again
Ronda Saunders led the prosecution with a blistering
assault on Norman and his intentions. Exhibiting the 'rape
Kit', and detailing Norman's consecutive visits to Amalfi
Drive, she told the jury that she believed that '...the
defendant was not going to give up until he killed or
seriously injured Spielberg'. Speaking about Norman and
his obsession, the director himself testified:

'I think he's on a mission. I think he won't be
satisfied until he accomplishes that mission
and I believe I am the subject of that mission.

Speaking of the attention that celebrity attracts,
Spielberg said:

'I've had fans, and I have had people who
have been real pushy from time to time. But
no one with handcuffs and duct tape and maps
and lists of family names. I have really felt
that to this day, I am prey for this individual.'

In an emotional final statement, Spielberg appealed to the judge and the jury:

> 'Your Honour, I place myself and my family
> in your hands, so that we may not fall into Mr
> Norman's.'

As Norman, flanked by sheriff's deputies, stared impassively at Spielberg across the court, occasionally yawning and scribbling notes, his attorney, John Lawson, attempted to dismiss the actions of his client as those of a person solely influenced by drugs. He claimed that while Norman may have acted in a strange way, what he did wasn't enough to make him a criminal. Using Norman's alleged use of methamphetamines as his main defence, he described his client as a 'mixed-up addict', stating, 'as far as I know, our legislators have not made it illegal to be weird'. He also claimed that Norman had only gone to Spielberg's home to act out a scene from his screenplay in front of the closed circuit cameras. Lawson claimed Norman had hoped that Spielberg might see him and thereby see the merits in his work. The jury was not convinced.

After deliberating for three and a half hours they found Norman guilty as charged. They decided the next day that Norman's sentence should also be based on his two previous convictions. The 'Three strikes and you're out' legislation, gives juries and judges the discretion to enforce an interpretation of the law which, if applied, carries the maximum sentence possible for a third conviction in certain American States. The likelihood was that Norman would have received three to four years for his behaviour towards Spielberg. But when the court reconvened for sentencing on June 17, 1998, Judge Steven Suzukawa handed down a custodial sentence of twenty-five years to life, the maximum penalty allowable. The judge was unequivocal in his condemnation of Norman and his support of the maximum sentence.

> 'The one thing about Mr. Norman that con-
> cerns me is that, frankly, I find his behaviour
> obsessive and frightening, and I think he does
> present a danger to society.'

Jonathan Norman told the California court that he was 'on a mission' and that he would not be satisfied until he had accomplished it. Norman wanted to hurt Spielberg because he was obsessed with him. He described himself as Steven Spielberg's 'Biggest Fan' but when arrested on his second attempt to enter the director's home, he had been carrying, as the prosecution put it a 'rape kit'. The only remaining question is what psychological aberration changed Jonathan Norman's admiration to violence and hatred?

Spielberg said after the incidents:

> 'Had Jonathan Norman actually confronted me,
> I genuinely, in my heart of hearts, believe I
> would have been raped, maimed or killed.'

CHAPTER THREE

The Kiss of Death

Most stalkers or those involved in an obsessive interest of one sort or another inhabit a delusional, disjointed and dysfunctional world. Believing that they can have a relationship with the object of their desire is often the central belief which supports their ongoing obsession. A belief that their victim in turn loves them can often be a further part of their delusional existence.

Jill Dando was born in Weston-super-mare in Somerset, England on November 9, 1961. Her parents, Jack and Jean, had a son, Nigel, shortly after they were married. Jill's arrival nine years later completed the family. They lived in a small house in Worle, close to Weston. Jill's early life was happy, uneventful and normal.

Jack was a compositor at the local newspaper, the *Weston Mercury*. Jean was a loyal and dedicated housewife. When he left school, Nigel followed Jack into the business, working as a reporter. The nine-year age gap meant that Jill had no real opportunity to become close to her brother. By the time she had grown up he had long since married and left home. She was close to her parents, particularly to her mother.

Jill grew up in the 1970s, watching television shows such as *Blue Peter* and listening to pop stars such as *Cliff Richard*, *Bay City Rollers*, and *The Osmonds*. In her teens she became a member of the Young Peoples Fellowship (YPF), the youth branch of the local Baptist church. The church was a reflective gathering of a small group of

Christians. The social events for younger members were tame affairs compared with what teenagers look for today. Jill was a gawky, slightly awkward teenager, with a plain face and glasses. She took part in many of the plays and sketches which the YPF would regularly stage. These were a chance to meet other young people but relationships were nearly always platonic with little or no alcohol involved – 'Fairly boring really' as Jill herself said later. From Worle School, the local comprehensive, she moved on to Broadoak Sixth Form College, where she became Head Girl. She was popular but a bit too straight for her teenage classmates who were beginning to experiment with drink and boys.

Jill never gave any indication of what she wanted to do with her life. She showed no preference for college, for travelling or for the career which would eventually make her a household name. When she left school, her father used his work connections again and Jill was offered a job as a cub reporter at the *Weston Mercury*.

Jill spent her working hours gathering information and stringing together local stories, writing on village fetes, church events, flower and pony shows. In the evenings she continued her interest in amateur dramatics, staging plays with a local theatre group. At this time she also went out with a series of boyfriends. She was certainly attractive to men but never seemed to get 'involved', in the long-term sense, with any of them. Many people commented later that Jill appeared to have fallen into a career she liked and that she was focusing on that side of her life for the time being. She gave the impression that love, marriage and children could come later.

In 1985 Jill applied for, and got, a new job at BBC Radio Devon, based in Exeter, about sixty miles drive from Weston. Despite being recruited as a programme

either, given her anti-social hours. She had to be at the BBC by 4.30am each morning! This cycle was only broken at weekends and by holidays. She also occasionally got to present a daytime show. It was inevitable that Jill would make better friends at work, amongst people who knew the demands of her job and who could make allowances for her crazy hours.

The line-up on the late 1980s version of *Breakfast* included soon-to-be-famous British current affairs presenters such as Jeremy Paxman and Sally Magnusson. Jill didn't really interact with the guests or with fellow presenters. She just read the headlines. This all changed when a new producer, Bob Wheaton, arrived on the show. His brief was to transform it.

In 1989 he re-launched the programme as *Breakfast News*. It now featured Nicholas Witchell, the often abrasive news anchor, with Jill Dando as his number two. Bob Wheaton, was infamous for 'shaking up' the BBC's more tired news formats. He was relishing the opportunity to put his own stamp on *Breakfast News*. The early morning news format had remained the same since the introduction of breakfast television in the early eighties.

Jill and Bob liked each other immediately. Within months their professional relationship had become personal. Bob was fourteen years older than Jill, had been married twice and had one son. Jill seemed to revel in the fact that he was a more worldly and knowledgeable person than herself. He also provided the male support that had been missing in her life for a number of years. While she had become closer to her father, particularly after the death of her mother, he was in another part of the country. Her brother remained in touch but his own family responsibilities meant that he and Jill had only ever maintained a fairly distant 'sister/brother' relationship.

Wheaton certainly became the pivotal figure in the 're-branding' of Jill Dando's television persona. His influence was quickly evident. Her style changed almost overnight. She adopted a sleek, professional look with classier, business style suits. Her hair also changed dramatically, replaced by a shorter, blonde cut. Most obvious was Jill's weight. Bob maintained a regular diet pattern. He encouraged Jill to follow his example. Jill's new image was noticed almost immediately. She started to receive fan mail and had obviously begun to stand out as a well-known news presenter.

A man who later became known as one of Jill Dando's biggest fans was Barry George. Barry was born a year earlier than Jill on April 15, 1960, at Hammersmith Hospital in London. The youngest of his parents' three children and the only boy, George had a difficult childhood. He didn't have anything like the stable home life Jill enjoyed. His parents' marriage was extremely volatile. Sometimes it was like 'a war zone'. Their marriage finally collapsed and ended in divorce in December 1973, when Barry was only thirteen-years-old.

Following his parents' separation, George's father abandoned his family and emigrated to a new life in Australia. The family home had fallen apart. Unable to cope, Barry's mother sought help with raising her children. A quiet-spoken, practical woman, Margaret George clearly suffered a great deal at that time but still remains intensely loyal to her son to this day. Barry was very badly affected and started having behavioural problems. He seemed to feel that his whole family had cast him off, especially his father.

To avoid what local council officials believed could become a very dangerous situation, at age fourteen George was placed in Heathermount, a council-sponsored special boarding school for boys who had emotional and behavioural difficulties. It was here that, what was to become, George's life-long obsession with celebrities first began to emerge. He told classmates that they should call him Paul Gadd. Gadd was Gary Glitter's real name. George continued to be obsessed with Gary Glitter throughout his school years, inventing fantasies involving himself and the star.

On leaving Heathermount in 1976, George moved back to west London to live with his mother. His first and only job was as a messenger with the BBC at Television Centre in Wood Lane in the late seventies. It only lasted four months but his fascination for the BBC and everyone who worked there lasted much longer. He regularly read their in-house magazine *Aerial* to keep up-to-date with anthing that was going on in the organisation. In the years that followed he stockpiled their magazines so that he could keep track of his favourite stars, including the young presenter Jill Dando.

During the 1980s Barry lurched from one fantasy to another. He was involved in a number of stalking and sexual incidents involving women. In March 1983, George Barry appeared at the Old Bailey charged with a sexual assault on a woman. Bizarrely the royal protection squad had captured Barry. They found him hiding in the bushes at Kensington Palace, wearing khaki, carrying a knife and a length of rope. When questioned by the police, Barry claimed that he was on a military exercise. He never had to explain why he was there and he was not charged with a separate stalking related offence because officers quickly linked him to the sex attack.

Police were not to know at this stage that Princess Diana was another of Barry George's obsessive interests and stalking her was part of his fantasy. It is extraordinary that, given the incredible public interest in the Princess of Wales at that time, the police weren't more thorough in their investigations as to just what Barry George was doing outside Kensington Palace. A man wearing military clothing found stalking a royal palace should have sparked a more intensive investigation. It must be assumed that the officers were satisfied with the fact that they were able to link the suspect to an existing crime and didn't speculate about his motives for stalking the palace. It is safe to assume, however, that Barry's actions were almost certainly directed at Princess Diana. The police noted that Barry '… appears to be a bit of a fanatic about the military'.

The Sun newspaper was later to quote profiling expert Dr Reid Meloy as saying that Barry George '…very much intending to harm Diana'. *The Daily Telegraph* went further saying that '… strong evidence had emerged to suggest that George had stalked the princess'. It said that in the same year as his arrest he had been stopped four times in ten months hanging around Kensington Palace. Much later it would emerge that he had been in the crowd at the Princess's funeral in September 1997. He had maintained an all-night vigil at Westminster Abbey in order to guarantee himself a good viewing spot. According to *The Mirror* newspaper he had held up a sign which read 'Queen of Hearts, signed Barry Bulsara, Freddie Mercury's cousin (RIP)'.

In court Barry used the name 'Steve Majors', a composite of Lee Majors and Steve Austin. American actor Majors had played Steve Austin in the 1970's television series *The Six Million Dollar Man*. As 'Steve Majors', George was convicted with attempted rape and sentenced to thirty-three months in prison. He served just under two years before he was released.

Meanwhile Jill's celebrity profile was growing every day. The BBC management no longer viewed Jill Dando as a utility presenter. As her performance on-camera began to blossom in tandem with her life off-camera she was achieveing celebrity status. She appeared at openings and launches and slowly gained a following. Every month brought a party and a meeting with a new famous face – heady stuff for a stringer reporter from the West Country. She was even introduced to royalty in the form of Prince Edward and became friendly with his fiancé, Sophie Rees-Jones. Jill loved it all.

Despite her recent promotion she was looking for a change. Working in any television job appears glamorous but unless you are very disciplined, breakfast presenting loses its attraction. Jill wanted to present BBC feature or variety programmes and started looking for auditions. Jill had to keep her ambitions quiet, since Bob, as *Breakfast News* editor, could veto her taking on any additional work and wouldn't want to lose his news anchor. In 1991, she appeared on *Safari UK*, with the veteran presenter Julian Pettifer. The programme was very well received, boosted Jill's image and looked well on her CV.

Her break away from news wasn't long coming. The very successful travel programme, *Holiday*, had become a mainstay of the BBC's winter and spring schedules. People loved watching exotic, sunny places on cold winter nights. Its main presenter, Anneka Rice, was leaving. The programme's new editor, Jane Lush, was looking for a fresh face to fill the slot. Jill Dando was suggested as the ideal replacement. Early morning shows are often viewed by television managers as a very good apprenticeship for young, up and coming presenters. If you're young you do it and then move on – if you don't take a chance when it's offered, you can be there forever. Despite the attraction of working with Bob, her mentor and lover, Jill was anxious for a change and the *Holiday* programme was a perfect career move.

In 1992, after three years as a morning newsreader, Jill left *Breakfast News* and started her new job. The only problem was that travel programmes, such as *Holiday*, are very demanding physically. And they require a high level of commitment. By the end of the first series of fourteen programmes Jill had travelled all over the world. First class or not, the programmes took an enormous toll on her, both physically and mentally. By the end of the run she was having second thoughts. She stuck at it, however. The money was good, and the travel, despite the long haul flights, did have compensations such as getting to visit places she would otherwise never have an opportunity to see.

By 1994 Jill's life had changed dramatically. Her relationship with Bob, which had been unsteady for some time, was virtually at an end. Despite their five-year relationship they had recently bought two separate houses. Bob bought his house in Maidenhead, on the outskirts of London. Jill bought her house on Gowan Avenue in Fulham, North London. The houses were miles apart. It was clear to people who knew Jill and Bob that he had played an essential role in her life at a vital time in her career. The problem seemed to be that Bob's previous relationships were in some way preventing him from making a more serious commitment. But Jill wanted a commitment. They didn't seem able to agree on where the relationship was going or if it was going anywhere. Eventually this became the catalyst for ending things. Their relationship certainly hadn't been helped by Jill's new job on *Holiday*. As she was constantly travelling and Bob was working to an early morning news schedule they didn't see that much of each other. Close friends had also commented on the unhealthy Svengali-like influence Bob had continued to try to exercise over Jill. He was fifty, she still in her mid-thirties.

Friends felt that relationships should be about love not be structured as management contracts. In some ways their relationship looked like it had become little else. Observers also said that Jill's increasing fame and independence meant that she had in some senses outgrown her older lover and adviser.

That same year Jill negotiated and signed a major contract with the BBC who had obviously recognised her popularity as a presenter. The agreement gave her one of the few 'overall' contracts the BBC offered. The contract essentially 'bought' Jill for a number of hours in the year. The BBC could then 'use' her in whatever role the two parties mutually agreed. These contracts are prized and are only offered to top BBC celebrities. The contracts often mean that the presenter can move from current affairs, to entertainment, to features programming, in the space of a week. The contract gave Jill a fantastic feeling of security. The BBC obviously wanted her to stay if they were willing to negotiate such a good deal.

Jill's agreed to work on the *Six O'Clock News*, *Holiday*, and take up a co-anchor spot on one of the BBC's most popular and successful current affairs vehicles, *Crimewatch UK*. Jill was keen to co-present the reconstruction and police appeal programme. The programme's former co-host, Sue Cook, left the show in late 1995. With credibility in current affairs, Jill made a good replacement. Thanks to her *Holiday* show fame she was now also a very recognizable face. The programme was still very much identified with her co-presenter, Nick Ross but Jill slowly started to build up her profile on the show. As her travel schedule with *Holiday* was still intense, she had very little free time.

In November 1995, Jill Dando was honoured in quintessential show business style. To her amazement, Michael Aspel appeared out of nowhere, clutching the well-known red book, and proclaiming those famous words, *Jill Dando, This is Your Life*. Appearing on a programme which she had watched as a child and which only featured household names told Jill that she had finally 'arrived'. But in many ways she had arrived on her own. Her relationship with Bob had ended a year before. Their split had made Jill more independent but also a bit lonely. To combat this, Jill surrounded herself with family and show business friends, chief among them the veteran singer Cliff Richard.

Jill had met Cliff at a New Year's Eve Ball in Vienna while filming a special piece for *Holiday*. In a surprise stunt, achieved amid huge secrecy, the *Holiday* researchers had arranged for Cliff, Jill's longtime heartthrob, to be her partner at the Ball. Apparently she nearly passed out when the secret was revealed. The two had subsequently become close friends. Cliff's other show business friends, such as Gloria Hunniford, were also a part of Jill's new circle. The social life Jill now pursued was just as 'safe' as the one she had followed as a teenager. Her friends enjoyed dinner parties and meeting up in intimate restaurants rather than high profile celebrity engagements. Then Jill met Alan Farthing.

Alan is a gynaecologist who returned to England in 1997 after an eighteen-month training stint in Australia. He'd been married for seven years and had recently separated from his wife, Maria. He worked at St Marys Hospital in London. Jill's cousin, Jenny Higham, introduced them. Jenny had noticed a number of similarities between the two and set things up. She arranged for Alan to attend a recording of the 'Esther Ranzen' show, which was being hosted by Jill during Esther's absence. After the show a group, including Alan and Jill, went on to a nearby restaurant where the two got on but it didn't look like a romance was on the cards. An invitation to Jill's birthday party followed but still no romance. It was only after an evening spent in the pub opposite Jenny's house that Alan finally asked Jill to dinner. Their first date was on November 23, 1997.

The budding relationship moved rapidly after that. Within a month they had spent a weekend in the Cotswolds together. A couple of weeks later, Alan asked Jill to accompany him to Australia for New Year. By early 1998 the relationship was in full swing. Alan attended Jack Dando's eightieth birthday celebrations in Weston and the couple were constantly seen together. In March, Jill and Alan were 'outed' by a *News of the World* door-stepping exposé. The article featured pictures of the couple, details of their romance and all the time they had spent together. For Jill this sort of publicity was by now an occupational hazard. For Alan it was a new experience. The article didn't affect their relationship but it warned Alan that he had entered a world were the, often intrusive, presence of the press in any celebrity's private life was accepted as normal.

Unlike Bob, Alan appeared to have no problem with commitment. Within a short time the two became engaged. For Alan it was a step into the unknown world of celebrity; for Jill it was a step into a world she had always wanted. At the height of her career she was now ready to look for a husband and family. As an added bonus, Alan Farthing was not from the world of television. Jill hoped that his relative anonymity meant that at least half their life together would be private and that she would broaden her life by having friends from another type of world.

Jill and Alan set their wedding date for September 25, 1999. Cliff Richard, by now a very firm friend, offered his garden for the celebration and volunteered his *Bentley* and chauffeur. After some discussion the venue was politely declined but the transport was accepted. Jill's celebrity status inevitably meant that magazines were vying for wedding photographs. A very difficult negotiation period with *OK!* magazine for exclusive photographic rights followed. Alan hoped the deal would keep all of the other magazines and newspapers at bay.

The wedding plans, as often happens between couples, were becoming a series of arguments, agreements and changes. They finally settled on All Saints Church at Putney Bridge for the service and Claridges hotel for the reception. They also had to sort out where they would live. The most practical thing to do was to buy a house together in the North London area. They were particularly interested in the exclusive and expensive areas of St John's Wood and Maida Vale.

Alan's house in Chiswick and Jill's house in Fulham went on the market at the same time. Jill's house at 29 Gowan Avenue, with an asking price of Stg£352,000 was quickly sold. This was no surprise as the road is in one of the most sought after areas of London. A young couple bought the house with the agreement that Jill would leave in July. Alan had spotted a house in Maida Vale. With a price tag of close to £1.5 million it was a bit pricey but within their range. The plan was to make the purchase by mid-April with a moving date of July to coincide with the Gowan Avenue sale. The sale of Alan's house wasn't going as smoothly but Jill had the money in the bank to cover the shortfall if it didn't sell. Despite these setbacks the wedding was coming together.

Jill's life was at a high point. Like most people, she'd often dreamt of becoming rich and famous but with no particular plan of action. Starting out as a cub reporter on her local newspaper the dream had seemed unattainable. As a working journalist she had received the sort of breaks very few are lucky to get. After years of hard work, unsociable hours, a massive image change and punishing schedules she had finally arrived. Jill's career was going from strength to strength and now she had also found happiness in her personal life. She was setting up a new home with Alan and a life of married bliss seemed to be on the horizon.

On Friday April 23, Jill returned from a two-day trip to Dublin. She'd been filming a report for a new BBC series, *Antique Inspectors*. She spent Friday night at home with Alan. On Saturday night they went to the Royal British Legion Ball and on Sunday Alan played golf and Jill just took it easy. This was a regular enough weekend for the two of them. It was the way they imagined their life would continue to be. They watched the first episode of *Antique Inspectors* on Sunday night. Jill happily answered calls from friends congratulating her on the new show.

Jill had a day off on Monday but lots to do. She wanted to sort out a few wedding problems, make some calls and get a new cartridge for her fax machine. She was also going to a Tomasz Starzewski fashion show at the Lanesborough Hotel at Hyde Park Corner with her friend, Anastasia Baker. Jill started out little knowing that this was going to be anything but a normal day.

Jill Dando's movements that morning are now fairly well documented. She got some petrol near Chiswick at 10.22am, picked up some paper in a stationary shop in Hammersmith, failed to sort out her fax and headed home.

By 11.20am she was seen parking her car on Munster Road close by her house as she dropped into the local fishmongers. A man saw her walking back towards her parked car at around 11.30am. Jill drove off and went straight home.

And then it happened. As thirty-seven-year-old Jill Dando walked towards her front door she was attacked and gunned down, with a bullet through the head.

There were no witnesses to the actual event but there were witnesses to sounds and sights connected to the gruesome murder.

Richard Hughes, Jill's next door neighbour, is a financial markets trader who works from home. He was well used to the sounds Jill Dando habitually made when she came home. Her car alarm activating was always the first thing he heard. He was upstairs in the front bedroom when he heard her alarm and then her footsteps on the front path. Next he heard a small screaming sound. This was 'out of the norm' but it wasn't the sort of sound to be worried about. In fact, he was later to testify that the sound reminded him of someone playing a joke. It was as if whoever it was had been waiting in the front porch to surprise Jill. Shortly afterwards, Richard heard the sound of Jill's gate closing. He saw a man passing his house going towards Fulham Palace Road. He presumed the man was Jill's friend and thought nothing more of it.

About ten minutes later Helen Doble, who lived on nearby Wardo Avenue, was walking by 29, Gowan Avenue. Helen was a Jill Dando fan. She always kept an eye out for Jill as she passed her house. She saw the *BMW* parked outside and glanced towards the front door. She couldn't believe what she saw. A woman's motionless body was lying in the front porch. Helen was horrified and rushed forward to see if she could help. At first Helen thought it was the body of a stranger who might have hit her head against the stone doorstep. On closer inspection she realised it was Jill Dando – injured and lying in her own doorway – covered in blood. With amazing calm, Helen switched on her mobile telephone and dialled 999 for the emergency services. She was quickly put through to the ambulance service who promised to send help immediately. Helen didn't know what to do next. She decided to get some more help and ran to a neighbour's house at number 55. They quickly returned to number 29 but there wasn't much doubt in their minds that Jill Dando was dead. She was motionless, her hands and arms were blue and there was blood everywhere. Just in case the neighbour ran to a nearby doctor's sugery. The doctor was out but the practice nurse rushed down to number 27. After a brief examination she agreed that Jill was beyond medical assistance.

Richard Hughes heard all the commotion and went to investigate. The noises he had heard a few minutes earlier came flooding back to him, especially the little scream of shock – it must have been a stabbing, he thought, because he had heard no gun shot. Who could do something like this to Jill Dando – and why?

Within minutes the ambulance arrived and the police followed shortly afterwards. The press arrived next. A major investigation was soon underway. The tragedy, quietly discovered by Helen Doble ten minutes earlier, had suddenly transformed peaceful Gowan Avenue into a scene of controlled mayhem. The emergency crew frantically tried to resuscitate Jill's lifeless body but to no avail. She'd been dead before Helen discovered her body. As the police began to cordon off the street Jill's body was taken away to Charing Cross Hospital.

At work in St Marys Hospital, Alan Farthing was just

sitting down with colleagues to discuss the morning's progress when his pager beeped, Jill's booking agent, Jon Roseman, wanted Alan to call him immediately. The press had already contacted Jon, wanting to know whether rumours about Jill being shot or stabbed were true. He asked an incredulous Alan if he'd heard anything. At first Alan laughed it off – after all, who would want to hurt Jill? Jon promised to find out more as Alan wondered what he should do next. Within seconds his pager went again. This time it was the casualty department at St Marys – two policemen were waiting in reception.

One of the officers, Detective Richard Quinn knew Alan and had volunteered to come to St Marys. Quinn told Alan that a woman, matching Jill's description, had been taken to Charing Cross Hospital from the house in Gowan Avenue with serious injuries and had since died. The two officers stressed that it might not be Jill. They needed Alan's help to clear up identification of the body.

Listening to them, Alan felt in his heart of hearts that it was Jill's body. He made two telephone calls – the first to Nigel, Jill's brother, and to Jon Roseman. Both men had already heard the news. *Sky News* had reported Jill's death despite the absence of any official announcement or confirmation. They were desperately upset and weren't particularly hopeful when Alan repeated that the policemen had said it might not be Jill's body.

At Charing Cross Hospital Alan was escorted into a small room off the main accident and emergency area. Alan nodded a simple yes, when asked to identify Jill's body and quickly left the room. In the midst of his shock Alan had noticed that Jill's head was wrapped in a large bandage of some sort. He wasn't sure what to think. He still thought her death was the result of a robbery gone wrong. He believed that someone had been in Jill's house when she came home and that she had been killed while trying to defend herself; or maybe someone had tried to rob her in the street and had turned violent when she had refused to co-operate, with the most disastrous consequences. Detective Richard Quinn's revelation, some time later, that Jill had been shot in the head took him totally by surprise. There appeared to be no motive for her death. There was no robbery, no break-in – the murderer just wanted to kill Jill Dando. Her death was an assassination. Alan couldn't believe it. He asked himself why would anyone want to kill Jill.

Jill was certified dead at 1.03pm at Charing Cross Hospital. Minutes later television newsreader Jennie Bond, a friend and colleague, announced her death on air. The BBC had been on standby for an hour and a half, waiting for the official announcement. Everyone in the newsroom was stunned. Journalists, hardened by reporting atrocious crimes from all over the world, wept openly; Never before had a story affected them so deeply and so personally. News staff said it was like the effect of the death of the Princess of Wales a year and a half earlier. The difference being that Jill was one of them, they had worked with her, laughed with her and now they were crying over her. Every BBC bulletin was lengthened to include expanded coverage of the killing. A special tribute programme was hastily prepared and transmitted that evening. The newsroom was flooded with tributes, including messages of sympathy from the Queen and the Prime Minister, Tony Blair.

At Kensington Police station the initial stages of the investigation were chaotic. Given the high profile nature of the case and the massive media interest, the station had been inundated with calls. As the senior duty officer in charge of Kensington's serious crime group, Detective

Chief Inspector Hamish Campbell was leading the investigation. He arrived at the scene of the shooting at about 12.20pm and was astonished to discover that the body had been removed to Charing Cross Hospital. Preservation of the scene of crime is one of the cardinal rules of forensic investigation. The clear exception to this rule is if a victim is still alive and has a chance of survival. In this case, the nurse at the scene had said that Jill was dead. The body should not have been moved.

The police had no choice but to work with what was left – the physical evidence of a shooting. The bullet shell was lying on the porch floor and the lower part of the front door was splintered. The post-mortem established that the bullet had entered Jill's head behind her left ear and that the gun had been fired at very close quarters. The bullet was fired from a 9mm automatic pistol. The shot may have been fired with the gun pressed into Jill's head, ensuring an efficient and ruthless execution while also muffling the sound of the shot. This explained why Richard Hughes had heard nothing following Jill's short scream.

Despite the initial chaos, the police already had a number of sightings of a potential suspect to work on. Richard Hughes had seen a man passing his window shortly after he had heard the scream but was unable to describe him in any detail. A witness then came forward to say that he had been waiting for a bus on Fulham Palace Road around 11.45am when a man, perspiring heavily, had joined him at a bus stop which serves two routes, the 74 and the 220. The man was agitated and stood around the bus stop for a while. The witness got on his bus when it arrived but the sweating man stayed behind. The sweating man was also spotted by a number of other witnesses at around the same time. A number of other witnesses also claimed to have seen the sweating man – some even said that they had seen him get on the bus at the stop although this has never been corroborated. Another immediate line of enquiry concerned a sighting of a smartly-dressed man, carrying a mobile telephone, who was spotted close to the scene.

By Monday evening, despite the initial confusion, certain facts about the shooting had come to light. The state of play as far as the public and the newsrooms were concerned was as follows: Jill Dando had been assassinated that morning with one bullet to the head. The assailant may have been seen running from the scene shortly afterwards. The incident could possibly be connected to Jill Dando's occupation but police couldn't be sure as yet.

The next day as the grief began to hit him, Alan Farthing agreed to do an interview. Throughout the interview, with newsreader Anna Ford, recorded by the BBC and 'pooled' with the other networks, Alan remained calm and composed. His statement summed up what those close to Jill Dando were feeling:

> 'I cannot think for one moment what could go through someone's mind when they do such a thing to such a beautiful, caring and well-meaning person such as Jill.'

Almost immediately the police released an e-fit of the prime suspect. The police knew that the e-fit was a composite of a number of sightings, probably inaccurate, but necessary to stimulate reaction and encourage other potential witnesses to come forward. At the same time DCI Campbell said the killer could have had an accomplice. He released CCTV footage showing a metallic blue *Range Rover* on Fulham Palace Road, speeding south shortly after the killing. This was the most definitive piece of evidence corroborating a number of sightings of a *Range Rover* on the morning of the shooting.

As Hamish Campbell's investigation team could find no particular motive for the murder they worked on the basis of 'actions'. Actions are effectively individual jobs following up witness sightings, calls, tip-offs or looking at existing information about known offenders or people with a criminal background. Thousands of messages led to thousands of actions; all cross-referenced and prioritised according to importance. Suspects were 'scored' according to a complex system that effectively downgraded personalities which didn't fall into the investigators' categories; For example, if a suspect had a criminal record with stalking tendencies then he would be regarded as a priority; If a suspect was black, tall and slim then he would be downgraded as he didn't match up to the physical profile. The overwhelming evidence suggested a white male had been involved. Priorities were 'scored' on how interested the investigating officers were in their activities and to what extent they fitted the overall profile. High priorities were those that scored between eight and twelve points. Anybody scoring below that was receiving less attention. Hamish Campbell only had a certain amount of manpower available and the public response to the murder was huge.

Three days after Jill's murder BBC security was increased after threats were made against John Humphrys, presenter of the *Today* programme, and against the BBC Director of Television, Alan Yentob. The BBC also announced that Jill had received a letter from a 'Serb source' two weeks before her death, attacking a charity appeal she had made for war refugees from Kosovo.

At the inquest a couple of days later, Hamish Campbell

disclosed that the prime suspect made his getaway on a number 74 bus. The suspect spoke on a mobile telephone before getting off at Putney Bridge.

On Tuesday May 18, *Crimewatch UK* featured a reconstruction of the murder. This was particularly poignant since Jill had co-presented the programme a month previously. Presenter Nick Ross, visibly moved by the experience, took viewers though the episode in painstaking detail. The show generated over five hundred calls from the public.

A few days later Jill's friends, colleagues, and admirers gathered for her funeral in Weston-super-mare. Sophie Rhys-Jones was among the mourners, as were Cliff Richard, Gloria Hunniford and many more show business friends. Jack and Nigel Dando, along with Alan Farthing, led the mourners. The people of Weston lined the streets as the cortege made its way to the small graveyard where Jill was buried in the family grave next to her mother.

Unknown to all those involved in this emotional farewell the most significant event in the Jill Dando investigation had happened in the preceding days. Unfortunately no one had really noticed. On May 15 a police 'action' had been logged to check out an individual named Barry Bulsara. He had been the subject of a series of messages from callers reporting his strange habits and behaviour. Needless to say, the police were wading their way through a lot of messages from well-meaning people on the one hand, to outright malicious people, naming friends and neighbours, on the other.

In the intervening years, Barry George had developed another passionate and intense celebrity obsession this time focused on Freddie Mercury, the lead singer of the rock band Queen. He became so obsessed with Mercury that he changed his name by deed poll to Bulsara –

Mercury's real name. As Barry Bulsara, Barry George pretended that he was Freddie Mercury's cousin. On November 24, 1992, on the first anniversary of Mercury's death, George hired a limousine and went to Freddie's former house in Kensington. He left a floral wreath outside the property with the inscription, *Your cousin Barry Bulsara*. Onlookers asked him for his autograph and he handed them business cards which read Bulsara Productions Inc.

On a business front Barry Bulsara had also pursued his fantasy lifestyle, creating a number of companies citing lead singer of the Electric Light Orchestra, Jeff Lynne, as a co-director. He had also developed a fixation with firearms and military memorabilia of all kinds. His particular fascination was with the SAS and he often used the name Thomas Palmer – the soldier who led the SAS raid on the Iranian embassy in 1980. He kept a number of guns, decorative and working, in his flat and hoarded items such as gun catalogues and instruction manuals.

Barry George or Barry Bulsara as he preferred to be known, had spent most of his adult live living in a dream world. He was obsessed with celebrities and their lifestyles. He believed that his fantasies could transport him to another existence where his talents would be recognised. It's clear that Barry George was a disturbed man, living a fictitious life through a series of bizarre fantasies. His medical condition was unstable. His life was unfulfilled and loveless. He was someone who felt rejection more than most.

The 'action' on Barry Bulsara or George would not be checked until the following year, over eight months after it had been filed. There are two main reasons why this happened. Firstly, Barry *Bulsara* did not have a known criminal record which meant he fell down the priority list. Secondly, the people who had rung in about Barry George had to keep his name anonymous. The calls had come from HAFAD, the Hammersmith and Fulham Action for Disability charity. Members of staff had rung the police giving details about an individual's mental condition but they were obliged to withhold Barry George's name because of the confidential nature of their relationship. They reported that a man had called to the HAFAD offices on the morning of the shooting, and that he bore a strong resemblance to the e-fit. They believed that he had a fairly serious mental health disorder. A number of calls had also been received from other sources which identified Barry George, but these were also anonymous calls and were downgraded. Plus the police had many different suspects to choose from and Barry Bulsara or George was not a priority at this stage of the investigation.

Midway through the year and under increasing pressure, the investigating team spent some time following a lead on a Fulham resident who had been known to meet women through Internet chat rooms. The man had tried to make contact with another J. Dando in the London area. He had apparently tried a number of telephone lines in an effort to track down Jill Dando. Hamish Campbell went to Australia to interview him but the lead came to nothing.

On August 3, the hundredth day of the police investigation, *The Sun* newspaper offered a £100,000 reward for information leading directly to a conviction. This increased the total reward on offer from national newspapers to £250,000. At the same time, following exhaustive enquiries, the police announced that detectives had no evidence of any link between any of Jill's former boyfriends and the killing.

September 25 was to have been Jill and Alan's wedding day. Three days later, Cliff Richard joined Jill's former television colleagues as they gathered for a thanksgiving service at All Souls Church, beside the BBC's Broadcasting House in London. Jennie Bond and sports commentator Bob Wilson gave the readings.

By the end of 1999, the murder team had spoken to more than 2,500 people and taken some 1,100 statements. As investigators faced into the New Year they could be satisfied that they were doing everything in their power to track down the killer but the lack of a real break was frustrating. The speculation about a contract killing or any connection to Serbian or Eastern European terror groups had also been discounted. Hamish Campbell had indicated privately that it was his belief that Jill was the target of a stalker in the months running up to her murder, adding extra weight to the theory that an obsessed fan was behind the killing. He was quoted publicly some weeks later as saying that his 'gut feeling' was that the murder was the work of a lone man. While no motive could be discounted, police certainly believed that the killer had not just stumbled upon Jill by accident. He was waiting for her and had probably been studying her movements for some time. Campbell was also convinced that dogged detective work would eventually lead to the killer.

The police 'action' relating to Barry Bulsara finally came up for review on February 24, 2000. Detective Constable John Gallagher started out on what he presumed was just a routine task. Barry Bulsara had been given a low priority. DC Gallagher visited the HAFAD offices and discovered that a number of employees there had met Bulsara on the day of the shooting. Some uncertainty surrounded the actual time of his visit but Gallagher was very quickly able to establish that Barry Bulsara was in fact Barry George.

A check at divisional headquarters established that George had a criminal record. In April 1990 and January 1992 Barry George was arrested and charged with indecent assault but neither case went to court. He'd also been involved in another incident where he was seen by policemen approaching a young woman and then starting to follow her. At the time the officers had noted in their report their belief that 'This man has previously followed'.

Barry George immediately moved up the list of priorities. But he was a long way from the centre stage of the investigation. The fact that he was described as strange and had visited a charity office on the day of the shooting was not in any way sufficient to put him any higher on the list of suspects at that point. It was on further enquiry that DC Gallagher discovered just how central Barry George might become to the investigation.

DC Gallagher called to Barry George's ground floor flat at 2B Crookham Road. He realised that the flat was only about a ten minute walk from 29 Gowan Avenue. A neighbour told him that Barry was Freddie Mercury's cousin. Gallagher left a note asking Barry to contact him at the station – the first of a number of attempts to make contact. Were it not for Gallagher's persistence and Hamish Campbell's insistence that every 'action' be closed off properly, Barry George could have slipped through the cracks, dismissed as a harmless whacko who thought he was a rock star's relative. His pseudonym would undoubtedly have added to the confusion. But DC Gallagher would not give up.

Having left a number of further messages for him, Gallagher finally met up with Barry George on April 11 at the HAFAD offices in Fulham. Barry's failure to respond to the police requests had moved him further up the list of suspects. His subsequent interview and a follow-up visit to Barry's flat at Crookham Road moved him even higher.

Barry George told DC Gallagher about his visit to the HAFAD offices on April 26, 1999. He said he had gone there sometime between 12.30pm and 12.45pm. He also told the police that he had walked to 'Traffic Cars' where he had been given a lift to Rickett Street. The police had received a witness report about a strange man who had arrived at the offices of the cab company 'Traffic Cars', Fulham Palace Road, within half an hour of the murder. The man had asked for a free lift to Rickett Street, near Earls Court. A cab had taken him there as a part of another job but the man behaved so strangely that the supervisor had rung the police soon afterwards. When the same man returned two days later his behaviour was still so odd that the supervisor rang the police again saying that the man, who he described, could easily be a suspect for Jill Dando's murder. Barry Bulsara or George was this man.

The detectives sought a special search warrant for 2B Crookham Road. They broke into the flat, as Barry wasn't there, and began a systematic and comprehensive search. There were boxes and piles of newspapers and magazines all over the flat. They found hundreds of photographs, including many of Barry with guns and other weapons. He had many articles and photos featuring Jill Dando and other newsreaders. He also had copies of the Jill Dando memorial issue of *Aerial*, the BBC in-house magazine. The flat also contained many items of memorabilia of Barry's 'cousin' Freddie. The technical team removed jackets, shirts, trousers, shoes and a wide range of military related material including replicas, clothing and photographs. Gallagher was still undecided – was Barry a genuine threat or a harmless fan who had worshipped Jill Dando? Gallagher certainly didn't feel that it was the residence of a 'normal' individual. It was clear that Barry George was worth taking another look at.

Barry was placed under twenty-four hour surveillance but without some concrete evidence irrefutably linking him to the murder, the police were unwilling to commit to an arrest. By early May most of the clothing found in Barry's flat had been sent for forensic examination and the contents had been all but removed. As the scale of the investigation mounted, Barry brazened it out. He avoided the police wherever possible and treated any undue attention as an inconvenience rather than proceedings which might eventually lead to a criminal charge.

In the middle of May DCI Campbell received news that evidence of a firearm, consistent with that found at the scene of the murder, had been found in a coat taken from Barry's flat. Barry had told John Gallagher that he was wearing the coat on the morning of the shooting. On May 25, Barry George was charged with the murder of Jill Dando.

A somewhat unusual jury of only six women and five men were sworn in before Mr Justice Gage at the Old Bailey in London in May 2001. They had one simple question to answer – could a serial fantasist, who was clearly living a life outside his real circumstances, cold bloodily plan to kill, and then execute a television presenter who he had never met and had had no contact with whatsoever? Prosecuting Counsel Orlando Pownall told the jury how the police had pieced together circumstantial, forensic and scientific evidence to prove that George was the man responsible for killing Jill Dando. 'There was only one man in the frame at the end of the exhaustive police investigation,' he said. He went on to recant how George's reaction to the killing had been totally out of proportion to what one might have expected from someone who claimed that he wasn't Jill's admirer. In fact, George had claimed that he would not even have recognised her. Pownall recounted how George had visited local shops in the days following the shooting, looking for letters of condolence which he promised to pass on to the Dando family. He also suggested to the local council that they should consider erecting a memorial to Jill.

The defence, on the other hand, built most of their case on the fact that the shooting had all, of what Michael Mansfield QC described as, the 'hallmark features' of a contract killing and that Barry George was incapable of such an act. Mansfield also claimed that:

> '... there is no evidence, none at all, that prior
> to Jill Dando's murder, this defendant had
> any particular interest in her'.

The damning evidence against Barry George, however, was the forensic evidence the scientists had found on his coat. The prosecution argued that it would have been nearly impossible to purposely contaminate the coat with the tiny spherical particle made up of barium, aluminium and lead. It matched samples found in Jill Dando's hair and on her clothes. A strand of fibre that matched a pair of George's trousers also matched a fibre sample, which had been recovered at the murder scene at Gowan Avenue.

The trial was detailed, sometimes long-winded and often emotional. The police and the prosecution presented thousands of pages of statements and many witnesses were called, all of whom were deeply committed to telling their side of the story. Throughout the trial it was difficult to ascertain which side was in the driving seat. When the verdict came, however, there was no doubt. The jury decided by a majority of 10-1 to convict George of the murder of Jill Dando. As he passed the life sentence mandatory in murder cases, Justice Gage said to Barry George, 'You have deprived Ms Dando's fiancé, family and friends of a much loved and popular personality'.

George's lawyers immediately indicated that they would be appealing the conviction. At the Court of Appeal they claimed that some of the evidence in the trial was inadmissible. They claimed, in particular, that the forensic evidence submitted relating to the particle of firearms residue had been contaminated by the police. In July 2002 the findings of the trial jury were upheld in a sixty page judgement. The Appeal judges said that looking at the evidence as a whole '... there was compelling evidence to convict him'.

The evidence had been both physical and psychological. Throughout the trial it had emerged that George had targeted Jill Dando, relentlessly pursuing her, although not in any public way. In the trial it had been suggested that Barry George had substituted Jill for Princess Diana, after the latter's death, as the main object of his obsessive affections. It was suggested at one stage that he hated women and that his ongoing record of assault and sex offending attested to this hatred. Orlando Pownall commented at the trial:

'Whether he harboured a hidden grudge against Ms Dando, believing her to have wronged him, or figures he idolised, such as Freddie Mercury, is impossible to determine.'

One of the most extraordinary things to emerge about

the 'loner' Barry George was that he had been briefly married during the late 1980s to a Japanese language student named Itsuko Toide. She claimed he had pestered her into getting married. Four months after the wedding she went to the police claiming that she had been assaulted by her new husband. She returned to Japan shortly afterwards but the incident served to underline the deep problems George had in terms of relating to the opposite sex.

During the investigation police had spoken to stalking experts to establish whether or not George was suffering from De Clerambault's syndrome. The syndrome, credited to the French psychiatrist G G De Clerambault, describes the main features of erotomania, a delusional disorder where the sufferer will often go to great lengths to be with the object of their desire. Barry George's behavioural patterns over twenty years suggested that he was a potential erotomaniac who needed to be watched. The murder of Jill Dando was the final tragic act in his life of fantasy. His fragmented personality had been heading towards some final big blow-out. Unfortunately for Jill Dando she became the target of his obsession and ultimate disintegration at 29 Gowan Avenue.

The assassination of Jill Dando stands out as one of the most public and horrific stalking crimes of modern times. In Britain most people remember it as the defining moment in celebrity vulnerability. As with the murders of British political figures, such as Lord Louis Mountbatten in the 1970s, it sent a shock wave through the national consciousness. But Jill Dando's murder was different. She had done nothing to attract an assassin. She wasn't a famous political figure. She was an attractive, popular, television presenter whose celebrity profile had increased over the years and who was viewed as one of the nation's favourite television stars. From her first job as a journalist in the local newspaper, Jill Dando had risen to become one of the BBC's most prized national presenters. When she died she was at the height of her career and was, according to most close observers, experiencing real happiness in her personal life. The questions remain, why then did Jill Dando have to die such an appalling death and how long had the man who killed her planned the assassination? To this day these questions remain unanswered.

CHAPTER FOUR

I Know You Really Love Me

The most intense forms of stalking behaviour are mainly targeted at figures in the entertainment industry. All modern day celebrities attract extraordinary attention and in terms of celebrities, movie stars are treated as royalty. It's not surprising then that they often have fans displaying a lot more than simple adoration. When a fan's interest becomes intense to the point of infatuation experts describe it as 'love obsession'. This description particularly applies to any stalkers harbouring the delusion that they are loved by their victim. Brad Pitt has come a long way from his early days as a college actor in the American mid-west. He is now ranked as one of the top five actors in the world; In terms of sex appeal and female adulation he is often ranked as the most desirable. He is an obvious target for a 'love obsession' stalker.

Born William Bradley Pitt in Shawnee, Oklahoma on December 18, 1963, Brad was the first of three children born to Bill and Jane Pitt. His father, Bill, was a quiet man, and a trucker; His mother Jane was a school counsellor. Soon after 'Little Brad' was born Bill got a better-paid trucking job in Springfield, a large town near the Ozark Mountains in Missouri. This was the only move in his childhood. Three years later William's brother Doug was born and two years after that his only sister, Julie, arrived.

Brad had an idyllic childhood in a typical mid-western town. Family life was happy, stable and secure. By all accounts, Brad enjoyed school and was a popular and successful student, socially and academically. His parents were committed Baptists and the whole family were regular church attendees. When he was six Brad joined the South Haven Baptist Choir. Connie Bilyeu, his then piano accompanist, soon spotted that he had an expressive face that was compelling to watch. She later became his High School drama coach and a major force in encouraging him to act.

At Kickapoo High School, Brad enjoyed sports, debating and school musicals. He also developed a keen interest in movies becoming a total movie buff. He went on regular weekend excursions to the drive-in theatre with his family and friends. He loved the movie *Saturday Night Fever* and any movie that featured Robert Redford. He would later recall that the first movie he ever saw was *Butch Cassidy and the Sundance Kid*, which starred Redford and Paul Newman.

In 1982, Brad moved 150 miles from home to attend the University of Missouri in Columbia where he studied journalism. It was Brad's first time away from his family for an extended period and his Baptist faith soon lapsed. He threw himself into enjoying everything college life had to offer. Brad had no problem making friends and he was a popular face around campus. He joined the Sigma Chi fraternity and got his first taste of fame when he posed topless for a student calendar. Brad's plan was a college degree followed by a job in advertising, preferably close to Springfield. This would in turn be followed by marriage, kids and a happy, if uneventful, comfortable suburban life.

However, towards the end of Brad's final year, an

incident occurred that changed his future plans completely. While touring in an old Buick his father had given him before he left Springfield, Brad was involved in a serious collision with a truck. Incredibly everybody survived the accident but, according to Brad, this marked a turning point in his life. He began to rethink his future. He abandoned his previous plans and decided to try something far less guaranteed or comfortable.

Brad left college two weeks before graduation and two credits short of achieving his degree. He bought a new car and headed for Hollywood to try his luck as an actor. He had enjoyed his amateur experiences and friends said he had the looks and the talent. Anyway he could always return to advertising if it didn't work out.

Brad Pitt was twenty-two-years-old when he arrived in Hollywood. He had $325 and no job. Like thousands of other aspiring actors he started working in low-paid bar and restaurant jobs to fund acting lessons. He also delivered refrigerators and spent time telemarketing. His first acting job, landed after a number of weeks knocking on doors, was not the sort of role today's adoring fans would associate with Brad Pitt. He was hired to wear a giant chicken suit and walk the streets each night promoting a Mexican food chain. He was paid the princely sum of $9 an hour. The sort of financial desperation which had forced him to accept the chicken job would lead to other similarly bizarre assignments.

A year later, in 1986, Brad was still persevering at acting lessons. He was also working part-time as a driver for a stripogram company – the owner of the company lamented years later that they hadn't offered him a stripping job! By chance he met a drama coach named Roy London. Roy realised that Brad's teen-idol good looks could get him places in Hollywood. He also believed that

Brad had the romantic-loner look of James Dean and an uncanny resemblance to the young Robert Redford. Like many young actors, Brad Pitt had heard this sort of talk before, and was slow to believe Roy London; but, by the late 80s Roy, now also Brad's agent, had placed him in a number of small parts and he was regularly attending auditions.

Brad got his first real break in the blockbuster TV series *Dallas*. He played Priscilla Presley's daughter's boyfriend and appeared in three episodes. He moved from *Dallas* to the daytime soap *Another World*. More small television parts followed including *Thirty Something* and *21 Jump Street*. Brad had taken his first steps towards super stardom and he was able to give up the part-time jobs at last.

In the industry it is generally believed that very few actors can make the transition from television to movie stardom. In recent times George Clooney and Will Smith are two of the most notable exceptions to this belief. Brad deliberately kept his television appearances to a minimum, just doing enough to make a decent living. His eyes were on movie stardom and it wasn't long coming. He continued working on television series and the occasional 'made for TV' movie before finally getting the break he had been waiting for. He was offered a part in *Cutting Glass*, a low-budget horror spoof. Brad got third billing, playing the part of an all-American, good looking, basketball player. As Roy London had confidently predicted, Hollywood loved his look.

In the end it wasn't through the movies or even the television shows that Brad experienced his first taste of worldwide fame. It was in an advert for *Levi's* jeans that was only screened in Europe. In the commercial Brad played a convict who escaped from jail using his 501s to lower himself from his cell. His thirty-second performance was a huge hit. Yet again it was his looks that attracted attention and made him an instant sex symbol.

Brad's next significant step was starring in the movie *Too Young to Die*. On set he met sixteen-year-old actress Juliette Lewis for the first time. Since his *Dallas* days Brad had regularly become romantically involved with his on-screen partners and Juliette was no exception. Despite a significant age difference (Brad was twenty-six), they lived together for the following three years. They both became the victims of their professional success, spending less and less time together as their careers developed. They eventually separated in 1992.

In 1990, Brad Pitt's career took an extraordinary and, some would say, fairytale turn. He did a routine audition for a part that was ear-marked for Alec Baldwin. Unexpectedly the part was offered to Brad when Baldwin turned it down. Brad accepted the role of a happy-go-lucky thief called JD in the movie *Thelma & Louise*. The cast included Geena Davis, Susan Sarandon and Harvey Keitel. The director, Ridley Scott, had high hopes for the movie even though it opened quietly. Before long *Thelma & Louise* was hailed as a modern classic, grossing over $45m and picking up six Oscar nominations in 1992, including Best Screenplay. Brad Pitt's role, for which he was paid a mere $6,000, catapulted his career from a Hollywood also-ran to a major Hollywood star.

Lucrative lead roles in a couple of eminently forgettable films followed. Then Brad came to the attention of Robert Redford, who had become aware of the similarities in their looks. Redford was looking for someone to play the clever, sensitive and doomed younger brother in his adaptation of the book *A River Runs Through It*.

The film was widely acclaimed and the kind of roles

that Brad had held out for started to pile up. In 1993 he followed *A River Runs Through It* with *Kalifornia*. In 1994, Brad starred in the period family epic movie *Legends of the Fall* with Anthony Hopkins and Aidan Quinn. That year he also starred opposite established Hollywood superstar Tom Cruise in Neil Jordan's gothic horror movie *Interview with the Vampire*. Both films were huge worldwide hits, making serious box office profits and proving, finally, that Brad's name on a cinema poster could pull an audience.

By 1995, Brad was staring, with Morgan Freeman, in the dark thriller *Seven* for a reported fee of $4m. This was his highest paid film yet. It was a figure that reflected his position in the upper-echelons of Hollywood's top male actors. This level of stardom was new territory for Brad but appears to be something that had little or no impact on the way he lived his life. He still maintained a bachelor style existence in Los Angeles, often walking to the local stores for groceries. He made the most of his single status, appearing regularly in the Hollywood hotspots and, consequently, in the Hollywood gossip columns. In terms of personal security, Brad Pitt just didn't have any. At this stage of his career it never dawned on him that he would be of interest to anyone other than the occasional fan. It just wasn't his style to hide himself from the rest of the world.

In *Seven*, Brad acted true to form and fell for his co-star and on-screen wife, Gwyneth Paltrow. Their relationship went on to last two and a half years. Most observers believed marriage was certain when the couple got engaged in Tibet during the Thanksgiving weekend of 1996.

Brad was also attracting other accolades. *People* magazine called him 'The Sexiest Man Alive', while *Empire* magazine hailed him 'One of the 100 sexiest stars in film history'. The downside of this acclaim was some unwanted attention.

In 1997 Brad Pitt had to petition the courts to protect his privacy. At the Los Angeles' Superior Court in June 1997 Brad's attorney, John Lavely Jr, sought to have the August edition of *Playgirl* removed from outlets nationwide. Brad was featured on the cover under the title 'Brad Pitt Nude' and the glossy magazine contained ten unauthorised nude photographs of the actor. Lavely told Judge Robert O'Brien that the photographs were illegally taken by a trespassing paparazzo (with a telephoto lens) while Pitt and Gwyneth Paltrow were on holiday in the Caribbean island of St Bart's. Lavely asked for a temporary restraining order that would force *Playgirl* to halt distribution of the issue and recall all copies currently on the shelves. Pitt was also seeking unspecified damages for invasion of privacy and infliction of emotional distress. *Playgirl's* lawyers countered by saying that the pictures were two years old and had been published on the Internet and in European tabloids. According to their lawyer, Kent Raygor, they did not commission the photographs. He told the judge that the shots were 'famous' and that a web site, featuring them, had received 750,000 hits since they appeared.

Brad won a partial victory when the judge ordered the publishers to cease distribution of the August issue. However, Judge O'Brien did not order a complete recall. Any magazines already out on the shelves did not have to be removed. Brad's case had to go on to a second hearing before the August issue was completely withdrawn and the publisher agreed to pay an undisclosed amount of damages. This would not be the last time that Brad would have to seek legal aid to protect his private life.

Brad's eclectic choice of movie roles continued with his starring role in *Seven Years in Tibet*, after which he was banned from entering China. His next role in the futuristic thriller *Twelve Monkeys,* co-starring with Bruce Willis, earned him an Oscar nomination and won him a Golden Globe. In *Meet Joe Black*, Brad teamed up once again with Anthony Hopkins. This movie coincided with the sudden end of his relationship with Gwyneth Paltrow. For the tabloids this became the big celebrity story of the day. Brad and Gwyneth were Hollywood's 'Golden couple' and the demise of their relationship took celebrity watchers very much by surprise. A few weeks before the break-up the tabloid press was speculating about the likely date of their wedding. The couple announced the end of their engagement by mutual agreement and called off their wedding. Brad released a seventeen-word press release to the effect. Their plan to work together on the film *Duets* was immediately cancelled. Gwyneth went on to star in the movie herself alongside 1980's rock performer Huey Lewis. By1998 'The Sexiest Man Alive' (a title, which had been awarded to Brad again that year) had found love again. He met *Friends* star Jennifer Aniston.

Jennifer Aniston grew up in Greece, New York and California. Her Godfather was the actor Telly Savalas, most famous for his role as TV detective *Kojak*. Jennifer studied drama at the Fiorello La Guardia School of Music, Art & Performing Arts; it later became better known as the 'Fame' school. By 1993, Jennifer had all but given up on the acting industry as a way of making a serious living. Then, in 1994, she was asked to audition for a television pilot called *Friends Like These*. Originally asked to go forward for the role of Monica, Jennifer refused. Instead, she auditioned for the role of Rachel Green, the rich kid turned coffee shop waitress. The rest is history. *Friends* is one of the most successful television sit-coms of all time, grossing millions of dollars for its producers and an estimated $1m per episode for each of its six co-stars. Jennifer had also become a movie star in her own right by the time she met Brad Pitt, starring in leading roles in movies such as *Picture Perfect.*

From the start of his Hollywood career Brad had remained close to his family and his childhood roots. The Press was usually alerted to a 'serious' new girlfriend if he took her home to Springfield to meet his family. His brother Doug Pitt owns a computer business in Springfield and his sister Julie has settled nearby. When Brad took Jennifer to visit them the gossip columns started speculating that the *Friends* star would become the first Mrs Brad Pitt. There were rumours that the couple had bought a palatial home together in Beverly Hills and a four hundred acre holiday home on the coast. People saw them as Hollywood's ultimate golden couple, living the Hollywood dream, combining glamour with affluence and talent.

The rumours were only partly true. Yes, the couple were spending most of their time together and, yes, they were looking at the possibility of buying property together. Brad, however, was still based at his home – an estate on Briarcliff Drive in the Hollywood Hills. Few people knew exactly where Brad lived. Oddly enough his house didn't feature on many of the maps of stars' homes, which tourists bought on street corners in the Hollywood area. Despite his tendency to wander about the area in which he lived, Brad maintained a very low-key existence. Very few fans had enough information to make the pilgrimage to the home of their idol. But one Brad-obsessed young woman had gone further – she not only knew where Brad lived – she'd already gone to his house, and in January 1999, she was planning another visit.

Nineteen-year-old Athena Rolando considered herself to be Brad Pitt's biggest and most loyal fan. She'd seen all of his movies, some of them twenty times. She thought she knew everything there was to know about Brad Pitt — where he came from, what he liked to do with his spare time, what food he liked to eat. Athena idolized Brad and had studied his every move for a number of months. She believed that she and Brad were suited to each other. It was much more intense than a normal relationship. Athena loved Brad, was devoted to him, wanted to marry him and believed that they were destined to be together. Most disturbingly, Athena was convinced that Brad felt the same way about her.

Like a lot of stalkers, little is known about Athena Rolando's early life. She was born in the rural state of Montana and spent the first few years of her life in Billings, one of the larger cities in the state. She subsequently moved to Spokane, Washington State, which is located in the upper north-west corner of the United States. Clearly a lonely person, it was later reported that she had not spoken to her family in six or seven years, suggesting that she may have left home aged twelve or thirteen. The reasons for this early departure are unknown but by the time she had targeted Brad Pitt as the object of her affections, her mental state had clearly deteriorated to the point of severe delusion. She confirmed later that she studied the actor and his life as if he were a college project. She had seen his episodes of *Dallas* and his one appearance in *21 Jump Street* and could recite the words of all of his movies, from *Thelma and Louise* to his most recent release at that time, *Meet Joe Black*. She had seen Brad on the television, on the movies and, it is understood, at least once in person, at a movie premiére. This was not enough for Athena Rolando; she wanted a one-to-one experience with Brad that would validate the love that she believed the actor harboured for her.

Athena was drawn to the house on Briarcliff Drive. She'd thought long and hard about what she would do if Brad answered the door. On Wednesday, January 6, 1999, she had gone to the house and just hung around. It was a nice day. She had spent some time in the winter sunshine waiting to see if Brad might appear but there was no sign of him. There was a good reason for that. Pitt was in the middle of filming *Fight Club* with Ed Norton and was also visiting Jennifer's relatives in Greece.

The next night, January 7, Athena was back at the house. She arrived at Briarcliff Drive in a taxi sometime after midnight. The driver remembered her as someone behaving in an unusual manner. Her dress was very strange too – she was wearing only a bathrobe and furry bunny slippers. She stood around for a while and then rang the bell but got no answer. Growing impatient she started to pace about, mumbling to herself. Eventually she clambered, with some difficulty, over the estate's eight-foot high fence. She looked around for a short while and noticing an open window she dragged a dustbin across a path and placed it underneath the window. She then jumped up onto the bin and scrambled into the house. Inside, she took her time looking around, eventually finding her way into Brad's bedroom. Athena spent some time in Pitt's dressing area; She rooted through closets and drawers and examined his personal belongings. She put on some of his clothes including black sweatpants, a green sweatshirt, a blue hat and a pair of tennis shoes. She later claimed that she had been 'cold'.

Athena had brought some of her own things into the house, including a book on witchcraft. She also had a large safety pin wrapped with ribbons that she later said was a 'doll' and was a gift for Pitt. She also carried several letters addressed to the actor. She spent most of her time in the house in and around Brad's bedroom, seemingly oblivious to the fact that she might be discovered. At some stage she fell asleep on the bed. Brad's bed had played a starring role in many of her obsessive fantasies so she relaxed into enjoying some part at least of her dream life.

Early on the morning of January 8, the estate caretaker, Richard Malchar, discovered Athena asleep on the bed. An intruder alarm had been activated and Malchar had arrived to investigate. He asked her what she was doing in the house. Rolando replied:

> 'I just had to see William. I just felt that it
> was something I had to do. I'd a strong desire
> to do that. I heard voices telling me to come
> into William's house.'

The use of Brad Pitt's baptismal name 'William' indicated that Rolando believed that she was so intimate with Pitt that she could use his proper name in conversation and letters. The caretaker called the police.

Officers Jones and Moreno were on patrol in the Hollywood Hills area when they got a radio call reporting a burglary. As the report suggested that the victim was holding the suspect, the police made their way to the Briarcliff Drive mansion at top speed. When they arrived Richard Malchar let them in and handed over Athena Rolando. Moreno and Jones were then joined by a number of other LAPD officers, including Officer Bennyworth. They cautioned Rolando and started some preliminary questioning to try to find out why she was in the house and why she was wearing Brad Pitt's clothes. Rolando replied, that it was '… hard to explain, but something was telling me to go to Pitt's'. Officer Moreno asked her how she had got into the house. Rolando explained that she had tried ringing the bell but nobody had answered so she climbed over the fence and got in through an open window.

More questions followed. Rolando said:

> 'I placed the gift [pin and the ribbons] on the dining room table. I looked through certain bedroom drawers. While waiting for him, I got cold, so I went into one of his drawers and got some clothes and tennis shoes.'

She said that she had been in the house since about one in the morning. When asked again why she was there, Athena replied that she had a present for Brad, 'I made a safety pin with different colour ribbons and I wanted him to have it'. She was unable, however, to explain the symbolic reason for the one-foot long safety pin. She told the police that she had also placed a card on Brad's bed. She said that she had been outside the house previously but had not gained entry despite trying a number of times. She also told them that she had left letters at the gate of the house on other occasions. The investigating officers found all these items around the house. They also found the witch's book in the bedroom. Before they left the house one of the officers took photographs of Rolando wearing Brad's sweatpants, sweatshirt and tennis shoes. The police then took her to Hollywood Station.

The ease with which Rolando managed to get into the house underlines Brad Pitt's attitude to his fans and his personal security in those days. Maintaining a full-time armed presence around his property, as some of his acting peers lived, had never occurred to him. He later commented about the intrusion and said, 'It doesn't surprise me. It doesn't alarm me either. It's gross and it's what I expect'.

Police continued to question Rolando at the station. They wanted to discover how many times Athena had been to Brad's house. They also wanted to establish the level of the threat to the actor. They asked themselves, was she just an over-enthusiastic fan or did she have the capability to cause Pitt real damage? Officer Jones asked her how many times she had been at the house. She replied:

> 'Three in the last two and half years. The first time was in September of 1996 when I left a note on his front gate. The time after that was yesterday.'

The police asked her how she had arrived at Briarcliff Drive. She replied that she took a taxi by herself. When asked if she had permission from Pitt or the caretaker to enter the house or even be on the property, she stated 'No'.

The police decided that Rolando could be released because the situation did not pose an immediate threat to anybody. She didn't seem violent or dangerous. She continued to repeat that she entered Brad's house because she was 'curious' and 'wanted something to do'. She told them that 'it's hard to explain, but something was telling me to go and be with William'. Officers charged her with trespass and she was released a short time later without bail, pending a February hearing.

Police soon established that the previous night's incident hadn't been Rolando's first visit to Pitt's house. In

September 1996, Rolando had left a pile of letters at the actor's gate, which he had described in a subsequent newspaper article as 'menacing'. One letter included an apology for placing a 'chant' on him and his ex-girlfriend Gwyneth Paltrow, several years before in an attempt to sabotage their romance. Athena refers to Pitt as 'Moon':

> 'Moon
> You and I here
> I am half band but make one complete song.
> P.S. over 3½ years ago I placed a chant on
> you and Miss Paltrow to break up.
> I was young and selfish ... I am sorry ...
> I think it would work.
> And your eyes have haunted me since.
> Even if Magic doesn't work ... I am deeply
> sorry.
> AR'

Athena had got her dates completely wrong. She says that she placed the curse '3½ years ago' but at that point Brad hadn't even met Gwyneth Paltrow. Who knows whether Athena knew this and was refusing to face up to the facts. Brad had a girlfriend and before that he'd had another girlfriend. For Athena, however, these were just temporary impediments to the more concrete relationship that she believed existed between herself and the actor.

In January 1998, Rolando was found by one of Brad's staff, lurking outside his house at 2am. This time she wore only a bathrobe and slippers. At the time she said that she was a neighbour and asked if she could use the bathroom at the house. She also said that she had a '... strong curiosity about who lives behind the gate'. On that occasion Athena had brought Brad Pitt a poem.

A young aspiring actress, infatuated with Brad Pitt, breaking into his house and sleeping in his bed (in his clothes) isn't the sort of story that stays quiet for very long in Hollywood. By the time Athena Rolando walked out of the police station the media interest was intense. Just one hour after her release, Rolando called a press conference in Los Angeles. She laughed and smiled and told the gathered reporters and camera crews that she was 'not guilty for anything' she had done. She didn't think she had done anything bad. She announced that she would still like to meet Brad in order to explain to him what she was doing. She warned Pitt, 'others may do much worse'. She told the press that she had been at his house before but insisted that her visits had been harmless and that she was merely on a 'mystical adventure'. She went on to say that if the tables were turned and someone did the same thing to her and broke into her apartment and wore her clothes and slept in her bed she 'would be quite flattered'. The tabloid newspapers and entertainment magazines had a field day; 'I got into Brad's Pants!' and 'My night in Brad's bed!' screamed the headlines.

Psychologists later studying her press conference took a more serious view. The underlying message in everything Athena said that afternoon was that because she had a crush on Brad Pitt her behaviour might continue. A recording of one of Rolando's interviews was shown to American psychologist Dr Staurd Fischoff. In a discussion on *CBS News* he stated that Rolando shared some characteristics with people accused of stalking. He suggested that Rolando might be envisioning herself in a loving relationship with Pitt. He said:

> 'She's almost seeing herself in this classic, almost archetypal male-female relationship

romance, she is indeed, this starry-eyed romantic.'

Fischoff also said that Rolando was isolated and this type of isolation is common in the profile of many stalkers, 'They have difficulty relating to people in the real world and they live it out in their fantasies'. Fischoff pointed out that the sign of a potentially dangerous fan is how close they come to the celebrity. He felt, '... penetration of the home is one of the most serious signs of a real threat'. He said that while many stalkers seem harmless, they tend to have a '... dark, fragmented part of their psyches'. In the study, *Stalkers and their Victims*, by Paul Mullen, Michele Pathe and Rosemary Purcell, they comment that in the group classification 'love obsession' stalkers, '... delusions [arise] secondarily as part of a more extensive psychotic illness, most frequently schizophrenia or bipolar disorder, rather than manifesting as a pure or primary delusional syndrome'. Fischoff said that while Rolando did sound coherent, she had, in his opinion 'a very shattered mind' which in turn can sometimes be a symptom of a classic paranoid personality. There was certainly evidence in Athena Rolando's behaviour following the incident at Briarcliff Drive to indicate that the expert's opinions were right on the money.

In the days and weeks after her arrest and the subsequent press conference, Rolando sought to benefit from her notoriety as 'the Brad Pitt stalker'. She showed no remorse or regret for her actions. She spoke to the media on every possible occasion and appeared on radio and television talk shows, using every opportunity to publicise her acting ambitions. She made it clear to all who would listen that she was an actress of immense talent and that she was already known in the industry among agents and studio executives. This could have led many people to suspect that the whole incident was an elaborate publicity stunt orchestrated by Athena to help her break into the acting world. However, an extract from the Hollywood gossip and review website *TheHotButton.com*, shortly after her arrest, tells quite a different story and suggests that she must have had a different, and possibly more sinister, motive:

> 'The Brad Pitt stalker who was arraigned on Friday? I know her. Young Athena Rolando, 19, used to be the hostess at a restaurant out here on Sunset Plaza called Chin Chin. She was blonde at the time, subtly tattooed, tongue-pierced and very beautiful. (Don't judge her looks based on the news footage.) In fact, she almost worked for roughcut.com at one point. She was looking for work, and I offered to let her work as a transcriber for some of my interviews, but she flaked out. She was probably out buying maps to stars' homes. She was an odd girl who didn't want to be seen as a typical Hollywood bimbo. She always told everyone she didn't want to be an actress. She would play the stock market, even though she had a low-paying job, always hoping to start a small business of her own. And now, that's all she really can do. If she really did want to be an actress, she is done. She's famous now – famously insane. And while that could get her a career in porn, the best choice is probably to leave L.A. and to start that life she talked about. Somewhere else.'

Meanwhile, Brad Pitt didn't hesitate to press criminal charges. On January 25, 1999 he filed for a restraining order against Rolando. His petition stated that while he was, 'an actor and film star, he is entitled, like any citizen, to his privacy and to be free of intrusion, harassment and stalking'. The petition went on to say that Pitt found Rolando's '... conduct alarming and her motivation and admitted obsession have become more ominous and intrusive'. In his declaration to the Court, Brad confirmed that he 'did not know the Defendant Athena Rolando' and that he had never spoken with her nor initiated personal contact of any type with her. He also declared that he had never invited Rolando onto his property, let alone into his home. He said that he was informed on January 7, 1999, that a woman named Athena Rolando had broken into his house. Brad requested that:

> '... the Court make an order prohibiting and restraining Ms Rolando from coming near me, my residence, my work place or wherever I am, and prohibit any other type of harassment.'

On February 10, 1999, Rolando arrived in the Los Angeles Superior Court for the hearing. She was prepared to take on her own defence and was armed with *The Criminal Law Handbook* and *The Dictionary of Legal Terms*. Outside the court she told reporters that, 'everything is going to be fine. She stated that the trial was '...just another fact of life'. Commenting on the injunction she said that she believed it:

> '... invaded some of my amendments ... I'd actually like to file a restraining order against Mr Pitt himself, to stay away from me.'

The sense that Athena was still suffering from her 'love obsession' delusion grew as the trial continued. She said that she had wanted to give Pitt a 'beautiful voodoo doll' and to talk to him about their relationship. She spoke of other famous couples such as 'Adam and Eve' and 'Romeo and Juliet'. Rolando said she had no phone, few friends and hasn't spoken to her family in years. She claimed, 'I wouldn't do anything like this again. It was a one-time deal'. The court granted Brad his restraining order. Athena was ordered to stay at least 100 yards away from the actor and his home and not to contact, annoy, harass, stalk or sexually assault him.

Back in court the next day, February 11, 1999, Rolando pleaded 'no contest' to the trespassing charges. She was placed on three years probation. She avoided a jail sentence on the condition that she underwent psychological counselling to deal with the incident. She also had to complete one hundred and twenty hours of community service with a graffiti removal crew. Judge Dale Fischer also barred her from contacting Pitt. Rolando laughed and smiled when she heard this. She told the court she had signed up with a therapist but hadn't yet attended any sessions; She never went to therapy.

By the end of the year Rolando was grossly in breach of the terms of her probation. Summoned to a probation violation hearing on November 8, 1999, Rolando told Judge Dale Fischer that she had failed to attend the court-ordered counselling sessions because she could not afford them. She said that she had completed four of the compulsory ten counselling sessions but couldn't afford to pay for the other six. She explained that she stopped going in August 1999 when her money ran out. She concluded by telling the court that there was nothing wrong with her. Clearly sceptical, the judge ordered

Rolando to show him receipts to prove how her money was being spent. He told her that if he found that she was spending money on unnecessary items, instead of the required psychotherapy, she would spend time in jail. He set a November 15 hearing date to determine whether she had violated her probation and to ascertain whether her claims of poverty were legitimate. She escaped imprisonment again by agreeing to recommence her treatment.

Little is known of Rolando's movements in the period following the hearings. Information about her idol's movements, however, was a different matter. On July 29, 2000, under a huge white marquee on a Malibu beachfront property, away from the gaze of the world's press, Jennifer Aniston and Brad Pitt were married in front of two hundred guests. The couple designed their matching rings and their wedding vows, promising to make their 'favourite banana milkshakes' and to 'split the difference on the thermostat'. The wedding reputedly cost more than $1 million; elaborate flower arrangements costing $25,000 and special brown sugar candles were imported from Thailand; a huge fireworks display was laid on and four bands, a gospel choir and a twelve-year-old Frank Sinatra imper-sonator, entertained the guests.

Athena Rolando or the possibility of other unwelcome stalker attention wasn't far from the thoughts of the bride and groom. They planned the occasion in consultation with security expert Moshe Alon, a former agent of Mossad, the Israeli Secret Service. He was hired to keep out unwanted guests, particularly Rolando, who, despite the judge's warnings, had still not attended her counselling sessions. In the same month that Brad was enjoying his wedding, an arrest warrant for $5000 was issued against Rolando. The city attorney's office said that the move came after she twice failed to appear in court to give an update on her progress in psychological counselling.

The likelihood of Athena Rolando doing anything else to aggravate Brad Pitt and his wife at some future date is limited. What is of more concern is the possibility that she might harm herself. Her stalking campaign against Brad Pitt has parallels in a similar case that was reported in the United States at the time. Forty-six-year-old Margaret Ray became a regular, uninvited, guest at the Connecticut home of television comic David Letterman; She was even found sleeping on his tennis court at one stage. Her series of bizarre love obsessional activities, designed to get Letterman's attention, began in 1988 when she was found sitting in his *Porsche* in Manhattan, New York. She claimed to be Mrs David Letterman and told police that she was the mother of a fictional David Letterman Junior. After ten months in prison and fourteen months in a mental institution on charges related to stalking Letterman, she died when she deliberately walked out in front of a train, close to her home in Crawford, Colorado. Athena Rolando as another failed 'love obsession' fixated stalker, could possibly face the same fate.

Most recently Jennifer Aniston and Brad Pitt have had to petition the law courts of the United States again; this time to protect a different part of their private life altogether. On July 18, 2001, the couple sued Dalmani International, the company that created their wedding rings. According to Pitt, the rings were his exclusive design, never to be reproduced. However, the company had been selling replicas, pretending they had Pitt and Aniston's endorsement. They had manufactured and sold 'Brad and Jennifer' rings in 18-carat white or yellow gold, costing about $1,000 each. In January 2002 the company settled. They agreed to halt production of the wedding ring, hired Pitt as a designer and Aniston to model his creations. It is easy to imagine that 'love obsession' stalkers like Athena Rolando, could be some of their biggest customers.

Some people might feel that Athena's 'Night in Brad's bed!' could be dismissed as a harmless prank or a possible publicity stunt but the motivation behind her actions needs to be taken into account. Athena Rolando, genuinely believed that the object of her attentions was as interested in her as she was in him. For Brad Pitt, Rolando's actions demonstrated just how far some fans might go to demonstrate their 'love'. It clearly indicated that stalking behaviour, if left unchecked, can lead to invasions of privacy and in Brad Pitt's case the necessity of protecting himself with a restraining order. As with many other stalker cases it will also have left him with the knowledge that Athena Rolando is still out there thinking about him and that, one day, she might decide to come back.

CHAPTER FIVE

Copycats

If a stalker bases his or her behaviour on the activities of another stalker it can be very dangerous. The fear is that the 'copycat' stalker may go as far, or even further, than the original stalker. Technology, especially the Internet, has given potential 'copycat stalkers' access to a vast amount of information. In the cases of notorious stalkers, such as Chapman and Cunanan, web site tribute pages are available, detailing their methods, beliefs and crimes. Once a potential stalker has found a target 'expert' help is at their fingertips.

Sarah Lockett is an attractive and talented news presenter. Born in Guilford in Surrey, England, she grew up in the small village of Whitley with her one brother and one sister. Sarah describes herself as being quite a studious girl and not at all sporty. She preferred to do her homework on the day it was given rather than waiting until the last minute. All her hard work paid off and she won a place at the University of Bristol to study French and Russian.

He first job after university wasn't in broadcasting, although she admits that this was her career objective right from the start. In 1987, British Telecom was setting up its premium line telephone service. The service offers callers information, such as up-to-date weather news, for which they pay a higher charge than the normal call cost. Sarah was assigned to the production of ski reports and telephone bingo. The bingo job involved writing scripts and producing voiceover sessions with the famous British actress Barbara Windsor. It seems like fairly pedestrian stuff now, but at the time, in terms of the telecom world, it was pioneering work.

Her break into broadcasting came in 1988 when she began working as a production assistant in London's Capital Radio. The station is the City's number one radio station and Sarah's initial duties included the compilation of traffic reports. After a year at Capital she landed a job at the BBC's London local radio service, GLR, again as a production assistant. In 1990 she was offered work, again on the 'wrong' side of the camera, with the *Six O'Clock* show on London's LWT television station. Within months she was producing and presenting short news inserts and reports and her natural talent as a presenter began to be noticed by her colleagues.

Gradually becoming a talent in demand, Sarah spent most of the 1990s as a freelance presenter and reporter, working with the Newsroom South-East division of the BBC's local television network and SKY television, the satellite news and current affairs service.

Her first full-time job as a presenter came in January 1998, when Lloyd Bracey, editor of *Meridian Tonight* asked her to front the evening news on Meridian Television as the anchor presenter. Meridian Broadcasting serves a population of 5.5 million in the South of England; the service represents over 10% of the UK's viewing public. Meridian's main studio complex is in Southampton. The company also operates a number of news bureaux around Britain.

Sarah Lockett worked at the Maidstone studio. It is located in an industrial estate, somewhat isolated from the more commercial parts of this thriving town. Despite this drawback, Sarah felt it was a good place to work. There was, and continues to be, a good deal of camaraderie among the staff. The building's isolation and the relative lack of facilities meant people tended to lunch together, either on or off the premises.

Daily duties for Sarah included the collation and presentation of the main news bulletin. Right from the start she had a very high profile in terms of the stations local output. Newsreaders, even in a small franchise area, attract their fair share of notoriety and attention. The very fact that a presenter is on the television, even for a relatively short time, day in and day out, is a guarantee of being recognized by the public. A daily shift on Meridian meant the occasional 'hello' or 'Do I know you?' for the presenters.

It's a flattering attention which anyone would enjoy and it is satisfying for a presenter to know that they have an audience and that their work, for the most part, is appreciated or admired. According to Lloyd Bracey, who was responsible for Sarah's news programme – 'It's a high profile role where people relate to the face of the presenter…. I think for the female presenter there's always the added feeling of the possibility of attracting unwelcome attention from male viewers as indeed was the case with Sarah.' The unwanted attention, which Sarah Lockett couldn't shake off, began in May 1998.

The first letter arrived at Meridian Television dated May 27. It was marked 'private and confidential' for Sarah's attention. It started,

Dear Sarah,

I don't want to offend you but your new haircut makes you look like a boy. Oh well, it will

grow back in a couple of months so don't panic.
. . .

The writer continued, indicating for the first time the
real purpose of the missive:

> '...I hope this letter does not offend you too
> much as the aim of it is to invite you out for a
> drink, etc. I have already blown my chance
> probably. My name is Jeremy so remember it.
> I am 28 am English and am a freelance writer
> on economics related things.'

'Jeremy' went on to be more specific about his intentions:

> 'I will ring you at Meridian (Maidstone?) soon
> to invite you out. I am assuming the Meridian
> show comes from Maidstone but could equally
> likely be beamed in from Spain I suppose. If
> it is, why don't you have a suntan? Oh dear, I
> am insulting you again.'

He explained that he was writing the letter while listening
to the English football team play a match against the
Moroccans. He finished with the confusing comment,
'With your new haircut you can become a footballer!'.

Sarah later remembered the first letter in which Jeremy
introduced himself. She felt, 'He just seemed quite, like a
sad, lonely type of person. It was weird but it wasn't
threatening.' Sarah gave Jeremy the benefit of the doubt
for a while, something she admits now that she probably
shouldn't have done. Certainly in retrospect she should
have paid more attention to someone who was displaying
all of the characteristics of an obsessive fan.

Unusually for what Sarah initially regarded as simple fan mail, the writer had made his intentions very clear. He wanted to ask her out, wanted to establish a relationship stronger than the existing performer/viewer one and was prepared to give his name or at least his name in part. The letter was more flirtatious than sexually offensive. Sarah considered it to be simply fan mail – no more than that. She had received letters of this sort before and they had come to nothing. Her instincts were to ignore the letter and she did.

Jeremy didn't take too kindly to being ignored – he never had.

Born in 1970, Jeremy Dyer was not a normal young man. He grew up in Ashford in Kent, a small town located on the main road from London to the coast. Distant and oddly behaved as a teenager, Jeremy did nothing to improve his social circumstances. He shied away from making friends with people of his own age and had serious difficulties with the opposite sex. In addition to his anti-social personality, Jeremy also looked odd; With his round, thick glasses and unfashionable, sloppy clothes, he didn't endear himself to the girls he met during his schooldays and later in his lengthy college career.

There's no doubt that Jeremy was a social misfit. It appears that he had no close friends and, by all accounts, he had only ever had one sexual relationship. He met Sabine while studying for his Bachelor of Arts degree. He appears to have followed her to Strathclyde University, where he subsequently enrolled to take his economics masters in order to be near her. The relationship broke up shortly afterwards. The reasons for the break-up are unclear but there is no indication of any obsessive behaviour on his part. In fact there is very little information available about the relationship, which would lead one to believe that Jeremy may have exaggerated the whole thing.

Jeremy went on to spend most of his adult life in education – never quite going anywhere. A brief stint working at a London based economics consultancy had ended quite quickly. He had been back at home with his parents since the beginning of 1998. By the summer he was doing nothing which could be described as gainful employment. He had gone for a number of jobs but hadn't managed to get beyond the interview stage. Somehow interviewers always seemed to feel that there was something unusual about Jeremy, something not quite right. Certainly no employer of any substance was willing to take a risk on him and Jeremy felt too educated and superior to accept anything menial. He was well educated – his qualifications including a Bachelor of Arts and a Masters degree in economics. He saw himself in a well paid position in an economics or management consultancy firm or the headquarters of a major international bank based in London, New York or Hong Kong. According to Detective Sargent Neil Parker, later involved in investigating Dyer:

> 'Jeremy seemed to get a buzz out of continuously completing educational courses... university courses. He hadn't had any permanent employment and it seemed that he was going from one educational course to another. It was obvious that he hadn't quite decided what to do with his life.'

Back at home, Jeremy was at a loose end. He was actively considering becoming a teacher but appeared to be spending much of his time mooching around the house, in front of the television or at his desk composing letters to Sarah Lockett at Meridian.

By early June 1998, Jeremy was on his third letter to Sarah, describing her as his 'Pocket Lockett'. He was becoming more specific with his suggestions and wrote his most explicit request yet:

> 'Why don't you show your bra every once in a while, or lick your lips suggestively etc.? Do you dare do this on TV?'

Months later, Sarah remembered her reaction clearly,

> 'He worked his way up from very innocent references to my cleavage and things to these weird and violent fantasies... he seemed to think that I was getting as much of a sexual thrill out of it as he was.'

The frequency of Jeremy Dyer's letters to Sarah Lockett increased. The letters were coming to Meridian at the rate of two, sometimes three a week. His state of mind became clearer. He commented on his obsession with Sarah in a letter on June 28:

> You probably think it's really sad... that I'm so obsessed with you, that I can't get a girlfriend or anything... I'm probably very good company and a great lover, and I do meet girls. A girlfriend I told you about before was so beautiful I could never forget her. But nice girls only come around once in a while...'

Jeremy clearly watched Sarah's programme *Meridian Tonight* every evening. He was able to comment on programme content, the clothes she wore and compared her with other newsreaders and presenters on the station. He even started a league table between the three main female presenters on Meridian, giving each marks based on looks, voices, and personalities. Not too surprisingly Sarah came out on top. As she later commented:

> '... he bought these kind of medals really with ribbons like Olympic medals, and he sent them to me and the other two female presenters, and I got the first Gold medal and the others got silver and bronze.'

He wanted Sarah to wear her medal as he'd '... know that its nestling in your cleavage and that they've slipped down your jacket and I'll see if I can get a glimpse of it'. He also wrote a note in which he compared Sarah to his ex-girlfriend and the ITV sports presenter, Gabby Yorath, marking each of them in categories such as 'sex appeal', 'performance' and 'personality'. He marked Sarah somewhat lower than the others, remarking that he was 'just trying to keep you on your toes...'.

More letters arrived. Jeremy's obsession continued to grow. His letter on August 9 outlined where his 'fantastic lover ego trip' came from. He mentioned his previous relationship with Sabine, but did not name her, commenting that he would 'marry in one second if she asked me'. Jeremy boasted of his 'fantastic love making abilities' but rather bizarrely commented 'which I will not disclose to you because you are still a perfect stranger to me and this is very private stuff'. He added that 'most women fancy me as I look so great (muscles and look etc.)'. Jeremy had decisively moved from appreciative fan mail to letters outlining the reasons why he would make such a good lover. But Jeremy wanted even more. Many stalkers are content to just watch their victims, getting a secret thrill out of the hide and seek element of the 'relationship'. This was not enough for Jeremy; He wanted to progress to the next level and actually meet Sarah. From Sarah's point of view the letter ended on an even more ominous note:

> 'Believe or disbelieve what you want from the above. You will definitely meet me sometime anyway, when I get bored of letters.'

Jeremy's determined campaign continued. Sarah later remembered one of the more unusual enclosures she found when she opened another letter. Jeremy had sent a photograph of himself but he'd cut off his head, presumably to hide his identity. Sarah found it '...quite a creepy, *Silence of the Lambs-ish* type of thing to do....'

On more than one occasion in this period Jeremy phrased his letters using a series of questions and suggested answers as his narrative.

> 'Now for another questions and answers session.
>
> Sarah: Jeremy, I'm concerned by the unwanted letters you send me, in fact I'm a bit worried. How long are you going to write to me and will you stop?
>
> Jeremy: If you're worried, you shouldn't be. I just fancy you. It's not that amazing is it?
>
> Sarah: If I spoke to you on the 'phone would you stop contacting me?
>
> Jeremy;   If that's what you wanted of course I would stop writing.'

By the end of August 1998, Jeremy's desire to meet Sarah in person had crystallized into a plan of action. In a questions and answers style letter he addressed the issue of whether or not he was a threat to Sarah.

'Sarah: But why would I ever go out with you, you might be dangerous?

Jeremy: Well, I'm not. Of course your safety is of paramount importance to you, but you could bring someone with you or check out who I am beforehand or even tell the police where you are and who you are with in case you're worried.'

It seems clear at this point that Jeremy was getting a thrill out of his role as stalker. Later in the same letter the Sarah character directly asked 'Jeremy' 'will you stop stalking me?' He replied 'No', and commented 'I'm a nice guy not a criminal.' Once again he also mentioned his intention to travel to Meridian. Jeremy continued to boast about his sexual prowess. When the 'Sarah' character asked 'Are you really a fantastic lover?', Jeremy responded with 'Yes!!!' and asked 'Sarah' 'Do you deserve someone as fantastic as I am?'. In character she responded with an equally positive, 'YES!!!' bringing Jeremy's sexual fantasy to the desired ending.

Soon after this letter Jeremy tried to make personal contact with Sarah for the first time. He called the Meridian studios just before *Meridian Tonight* went on-air. A programme assistant intercepted the call. Unsure of what to do with this intense man who insisted on speaking to Sarah, she passed the call on to the programme editor, Lloyd Bracey. They had quite a long conversation.

Jeremy wanted to speak to Sarah, no one else would do and he was prepared to wait. According to Bracey in a subsequent interview:

> 'He wouldn't accept from me or anyone else that she didn't want to have contact with him'.

In any television station it is next to impossible to get through to a newscaster close to transmission time, unless you have a direct line. In Meridian all calls, other than those dialled through to direct extensions, are routed through the switch — a number Jeremy had tried many times before.

Jeremy referred to his conversation with Lloyd in his next letter:

> 'He seems a nice enough guy. I said I would ring back on Thursday to find out whether you would be willing to speak to me. This sounds far too complicated for my liking. It was not my intention to really involve other members of Meridian in the contact I have with you. I certainly don't expect to have to go through the editor to find out if I can speak to you…. maybe everybody in the Meridian office had read all letters. That is a good reason for not personalizing them with my name and address…. I'm sure you're aware, many women are terrorised, humiliated, assaulted, raped etc. … it is not my intention to hassle you at all.'

If he couldn't talk to Sarah by telephone it was clear that Jeremy would have to take the matter further and pay a call in person.

On a warm summer's evening in late August 1998, Jeremy made the journey from his home to the Meridian studios in Maidstone. Putting his bicycle on the train, he went north to Maidstone East, and cycled to the studios. His entry into the building was made remarkably easy when the security guard buzzed a group of cleaners through an automatic gate onto the premises. Jeremy tagged along with them and then spent some time speaking to the security guard but got no further than the reception area. He told the guard that he had an appointment and was waiting for Sarah. She remembered:

> 'A security guard had said that I lived in Hastings and that I was single, I think at the time I was already engaged. So the Security Guard got it wrong because I didn't live in Hastings.'

Police later discovered that based on this information Jeremy bought the electoral roll for Hastings to find Sarah's address. If the security guard had given Jeremy more accurate information events could have become much more serious. Sarah certainly felt that the temperature of the unusual 'relationship' between potential suitor and presenter rose substantially from that point. She felt that it was 'spooky' that Jeremy had travelled all the way to the studios on the off-chance of meeting her.

By September 1998, Jeremy had finally decided that teaching was the career for him. He enrolled in an one-year teacher training programme at Warwick University. The University is sited on the southern side of Coventry. The course required a full-time commitment and a move to the Midlands. Not for the first time, Jeremy was embarking on a new career path. It might also provide him with an opportunity to meet some new people. Evidently he had also decided that he would leave his existing life behind to pursue this new goal. In his last letter to Sarah before his departure, Jeremy finally identified himself, enclosing his full name and address. He wrote:

> 'I'm going away now so I won't be writing to you anymore, but if you want to write to me I'm going to take a bold move and give you my name and address. So if you want to report me to the police, it's all up front. I can't be a stalker now can I?'

According to Detective Neil Parker:

> 'It was almost as if he was saying to Sarah – you control this. If you want me to stop, you know who I am, you know where I am, write and tell me.'

Jeremy's decision to 'come out' at this stage is unusual for stalkers but it does demonstrate the somewhat naïve nature of his approach. In his mental state he may have seriously deluded himself that he did, in fact, have a real chance of beginning and sustaining a relationship with Sarah. He obviously felt comfortable enough to 'formally' introduce himself to someone he now clearly regarded as more than just a pen pal.

Sarah took the opportunity to write and thank Jeremy for his interest in her programme. She enclosed a signed photo, 'To Jeremy, best wishes, Sarah', asked him not to contact the studio again and wished him good luck in the future. Jeremy wrote back saying '…it's been fun, I won't bother you any more...' Sarah was relieved to think that the episode was closed.

However, a few weeks later another letter arrived from Jeremy, 'You know I said my last letter was the last letter, well it's not'. The letters started coming again. Out of almost 18,000 students at the university Jeremy had obviously had little success in meeting new people. He had managed to hold out for three months. Whether he found another interest for his attentions in the meantime is unknown, but by December he was back writing to Sarah:

> 'Do you like having someone giving you this attention like I am? Every celebrity needs a stalker – Oh well there are good stalkers and bad stalkers. And you my dear are lucky enough to get a good one who sends you nice presents and writes you nice things – it doesn't do your image much harm to have someone stalking you like this....'

According to Sarah:

> 'He seemed to think that being my stalker, as he called himself, was a good thing for me because it meant... I was a proper celebrity because I now even had my own personal stalker – and wasn't it lucky that he was a good one who had my best interests at heart and wouldn't harm me. Equally in other letters the tone would be completely different or more threatening, or more off the wall or weird – you didn't know which way he was going to go.'

Jeremy embraced his role as Sarah's stalker, clearly feeling that the 'relationship' was to their mutual benefit. After all the various university courses and degrees he had finally found a role in life that gave him a sense of purpose.

> 'I enjoy stalking you and I hope you enjoy being stalked – when you asked me not to ring you at work I haven't done since, have I? So who is doing the controlling here, you are. ... This is what makes this such fun. You can consent to being stalked, and I can stalk you darling. In fact it's even nicer that you can accept what I am doing – it makes it even more exciting. We can explore the boundaries of stalking together without anyone ever knowing – unless you want them to.'

The strong and deliberate references to stalking were starting to worry Sarah. She found them threatening but Jeremy seemed to think she was enjoying it. Certainly in terms of the letters to date this was the first time Jeremy had mentioned stalking directly. In fact the overt nature of the reference is very unusual. Stalkers, particularly erotomaniacs, are usually so consumed by their actions that they cannot separate what they are doing into a defined behavioural pattern. To the stalker, what he or she is doing is just another part of their normal daily activities – directing their attentions towards the object of their desire. Jeremy's letters varied from the affectionate to the threatening, always containing some thinly veiled reference to violence or physical or psychological harm of some sort. He was happy to have joined the exclusive stalking club.

'Always remember the golden rule of all stalkers, which I've just invented – If your stalker
walks during your sleeping hours, is he your
dream, or your nightmare? If you can choose
then be sure to kiss him goodnight before you
go to bed, and he will be your dream for as
long as you continue to kiss him goodnight.'

From Jeremy's point of view his first visit to Meridian
had been a disaster. Not only had he failed to meet his
idol – now her colleagues knew all about him and what
he looked like. Jeremy took time out of his teacher-training
course and made a visit home to Kent in early December.
He decided to visit the Meridian studios again. He detailed
his activities in a letter he sent Sarah on December 4,
1998:

'Let me tell you a story. One day a man went
to Maidstone with a pocket TV and his little
binoculars... He knew the pretty lady was close
by so he hid somewhere in case she saw him.
He was well prepared with his pocket TV and
binoculars to see the pretty princess when she
left Meridianland after the news.'
     After waiting a while in the secret place,
watching the princess on his pocket TV, he
saw her come out of the Meridianland palace
and walk across to her little black sports car.
She zoomed off as quick as can be. What do
you think of the story?'

It later transpired in police interviews and from witness
accounts that Jeremy had spent quite some time sitting
on a wall outside the studio building watching the news

on a portable television handset. He also carried a set of small field binoculars that he used to spot people coming in and out of the building. Wary of the security guards, Jeremy was not going to try to enter the building in case they would carry out their previous threat and call the police. He had planned to approach Sarah in the car park after her news-reading shift. He seemed to lose his nerve at the last moment.

Jeremy was keeping his distance, but Sarah found this bizarre behaviour even more threatening. He was tracking her every move, knew where she parked, knew her car and more importantly knew her number plate. Jeremy saw himself as a dedicated stalker so Sarah had to consider the possibility that he would try to track her down through her car. Sarah later commented, it gave her:

> '... a very spooky, hairs on the back of your neck type of feeling, to know that he had been there watching me and if he'd wanted to pounce there would be nothing I could do about it.'

Police later found evidence that there was substance behind Jeremy's claims. They uncovered an accurate car park plan, identifying Sarah's parking space, proving that Jeremy had definitely been at the studios that evening.

When the letters recommenced in December 1998, there was something bolder, more sinister and more threatening about their content. Jeremy confided to Sarah that he had often thought that he might be a serial killer. In examining the letters now the somewhat frivolous and almost pathetically innocent nature of the content of the early ones would, understandably, have led Sarah to discount them as the work of a lonely fan. Sarah found the mention of serial killing equally unalarming at the time. After all, the behaviour of the man she now knew to be Jeremy Dyer, could hardly be compared to that of Peter Sutcliffe, the Yorkshire Ripper or the killing sprees of murderers such as 'The Son of Sam' or the infamous Ted Bundy. Jeremy had already revealed himself by giving his full name and address. If he was a serial killer he was 'keeping it quiet' in a very strange way.

> 'I will now list some points about me which you can categorise as positive or negative – see which predominates. I have an economics degree as well as a BA. I used to be a fantastic lover. I stalked an ex-girlfriend for a long time. I have fantasised about becoming a serial killer.'

It is fair to assume that two of the points Jeremy made in this December letter were invented, possibly out of bravado. Jeremy was warming to his subject and wanted to demonstrate that he was a stalker with a purpose. He may have stalked his ex-girlfriend but no charges were ever pressed against him, so there is no proof that any other stalking even happened. His alleged 'fantasies' about stepping up his obsessive activity to the point where he might kill were probably just that – fantasies. Jeremy was a deluded individual, living in his own delusional world. He wrote to Sarah, talking about her breasts and other physical characteristics, describing what he would like to 'do' to her. It remains to be seen, however, what Jeremy might have been capable of saying, let alone 'doing' if he'd actually ever come face-to-face with her.

Sarah clearly remembered his first references to serial killing:

'He kind of invented different aliases for himself. "Mr Chuckles" and "The Cleaner", and these were different types of serial killers'. He talked about which he was most like and he thought that he was most like the cleaner and he rated them according to different factors — there was the fear factor, and the intelligence factor and sex-appeal and how mentally ill they were. He didn't think that he was mentally ill at all, but his intelligence was ten out of ten and his sex appeal was ten out of ten. So this was part of his narcissism, he wasn't content just to be a serial killer, he also had to be all of these split personalities, all of these sorts of serial killers.'

According to Sarah, although she did not recognise it at the time, 'It was no longer about me presenting the programme and him being a viewer. It was about this whole other fantasy world that he had entered.'

The frequency and the bizarre tone of Jeremy's letters increased throughout early 1999. Sarah felt that Jeremy '... was totally obsessed with me 24 hours a day'. On January 23, Jeremy hypothesized on the relationship between the stalker and the stalked.

'A stalker is someone who usually seeks your attention in some way and therefore will try even harder to contact you, meet you etc. The nature of stalking is one of a lack of relationship with the person you are stalking. ... What I mean by this is e.g.; if I saw you each week or met you regularly I couldn't send letters or write the things I write etc. because I would

> have some (social) relationship with you. I don't have that with you which makes it easy to carry on like this. Do you understand what I mean? ... Whatever the situation, I will find out which jacket shows your breasts off best and write to you at Easter.'

References to Sarah's attractiveness and figure, her breasts in particular, had featured from the start of Jeremy's letters. In his subsequent interviews with the police Jeremy admitted that he had had sexual fantasies about Sarah. There is no evidence of Jeremy ever having behaved like this before so it is difficult to assess how far he would have taken his "fantasies".

By February 24, Jeremy was talking about his dreams and sexual fantasies in much clearer and stronger language. He dreamt that he was in the studio with Sarah trying to look down her bra. He complained, 'Why can't I dream of having sex with you? Bloody dreams, can't even do what you want in them'. There's no doubt that Jeremy was trying to, in some sense, up the ante. The increasingly disturbing nature of the content of the letters was having an effect on Sarah. She believed that Jeremy had become immersed in sexual fantasies where he saw her in roles such as, a mythical beast, having sex with three men at the same time and then killing them. Sarah felt his ideas got '... a lot more graphic and hardcore'. All of these fantasies were contained in the letters sent in the first part of 1999.

> '8th March
>
> Hi! Guess what? I've just discovered an interesting thing about your name. If you

> reverse the name Sarah it becomes… HaraS.
> That's only one letter away from the word
> Harass as in harassment. Reading it out loud
> sounds exactly the same. HaraS Sarah. My
> true purpose is finally revealed to me. Harass
> Sarah.'

The thought that the same person was obsessed with her
on an almost full-time basis, despite having never met
her, was difficult to come to terms with. Lloyd Bracey,
Sarah's editor, was aware of the situation from the start
but saw no adverse impact on her television performance.
He believed that anyone receiving similar letters would
find the attention 'quite a bit bothersome'. He discussed
passing the letters on to the police with Sarah but they
both believed that the matter wasn't that serious.

Sarah herself, however, felt a growing sense of
awareness of Jeremy in her nightly news presentations.
She later commented:

> 'I found myself thinking about him during
> the programmes that I was presenting – which
> I had to just block out, because at the time
> you just have to be professional and you just
> have to do the interview that you're doing or
> read the link that you're doing, or whatever.
> But I, looking at the camera lens, thought –
> he's watching me now.'

At Easter, back at home on a break from his course,
Jeremy tried to revive what he clearly considered to be a
dying relationship.

'OK let's have a strategy meeting. How is our

stalking experience going? What do we want
out of Easter?

> Re-establish our relationship
> Launch 'operation Lockett watch – Easter'
> Send some letters, presents etc
> Watch Sarah on M.Ton (Meridian Tonight)
> Other'

Jeremy goes on to give Sarah an option to end the
'relationship'. Again he is looking for some sort of a sign
to do with her clothes:

> 'If you (Sarah Lockett) wear your blue jacket
> with the split down the front on Meridian
> Tonight on Friday, 9th April – I (Jeremy) will
> stop all contact with you... forever. If you don't
> wear it I will continue to write... forever.

> ...all I am doing is giving you an opportunity
> to decide things for yourself. Your views are
> valid and to be respected, as are mine. Okay,
> that's the end of our strategy meeting.'

By now the letters had topped fifty, an average of two
a week since Jeremy started his stalking campaign. He
decided to make a third visit to Meridian. He arrived at
the studios in the evening and claimed that he had an
appointment to meet Sarah. He talked his way into the
studio but then one of the security guards realized who
he was and threw him out. Sarah wasn't due to broadcast
that evening and there is some confusion as to whether
or not Jeremy was aware of this. There is no doubt in
Sarah's mind; judging by the content of the more recent

letters she was positive that Jeremy had reached a point where he wanted to meet her that night. He may have been acting on impulse which is why he didn't check out if she would definitely be there or not but his intentions were clear. As far as Sarah was concerned, 'he was getting bolder and bolder'.

The incident encouraged Lloyd Bracey to take further action. To the outsider it might seem that both he and Sarah waited too long to try to bring the matter to a head; But in a busy news station, the letters, however graphic they were becoming, were still regarded as the work of a harmless fan. Bracey thought that he might be able to intervene and wrote a letter to Jeremy. He told Jeremy, '... this isn't getting you anywhere, please will you stop and if you don't stop we'll have to call the police'. The note was a courteous, but firm, reiteration of the verbal rebuffs previously given by Bracey. Jeremy had also received warnings from other members of the Meridian news team and the security guards. Bracey continued:

> 'I hope that you will realise that you are wasting your time and effort and causing a nuisance. I feel we have dealt with you very courteously thus far. Please be aware that we will not hesitate to involve the police if you persist.'

The warning made Jeremy back off, but only for a week or two. He made his feelings on the matter very clear to Sarah.

> 'Before you turn me over to the police – to get life in prison – for posting chocolates to a lady, remember you will be wrecking my whole

life completely… I am not a proper stalker, I
just fancy you a bit….I thought you were a nice
person (and still do). Maybe I will write (to
the editor) explaining things.'

A further note had a more sinister tone to it and
contained a frightening and threatening promise:

'In the summer I will definitely come looking
for you. Finders keepers, losers PETER'S.
Come summer '99, you're mine. When I come
back, I'll teach you a lesson.'

Jeremy obviously knew that Sarah had a boyfriend
and even acknowledged that his name was Peter. Jeremy
had read about him in a feature on Sarah in a local
newspaper. The feature had also provided some other
useful information. Sarah, it said, lived in Tonbridge.
Jeremy had trawled his way through the Tonbridge
electoral register looking for Lockett, S. If he arrived at
her house it would be difficult for Sarah to avoid him. As
far as Jeremy was concerned Peter was an irrelevance –
Sarah wasn't married to him and, after all, Jeremy felt he
was conducting a far more intense relationship with Sarah
than Peter ever could.

In Coventry, Jeremy had a problem. He was now living
too far away to receive Sarah's live television broadcasts.
He needed to find a new way to fuel his obsession. He
placed an advertisement in the local paper in Kent stating
that he would pay cash to anyone who was willing to
video episodes of *Meridian Tonight* for him each day.
Two people responded to his advertisement. The job went
to a young man named Ian who received £30 plus the
cost of the tapes each week. Jeremy itemised in great

detail the times of the day he wanted recorded, times when Sarah would most likely be appearing on the television. He also paid to have the tapes sent to him in Coventry. This clearly illustrates the intensity of his obsession with Sarah. Fifty letters and over a year later his obsession was still as strong as ever. Jeremy was obviously proud of his sense of commitment. In a letter Jeremy sent before he departed for Warwick again he revealed to his idol that he had organised for her nightly show to be recorded:

> 'By the way before I forget. I will be employing someone in Kent to post all your April, May and June Meridian Tonights to me in Coventry. I will tell them it is for a University of Warwick news database. They will never suspect a thing. I will tell the person we need a regional news gatherer to cover the Kent region.'

According to Detective Neil Parker, subsequent investigations revealed that Jeremy had told Ian this exact story. Ian had no idea what was going on. He completely believed Jeremy's 'cover story' that he was doing a media course at the University of Warwick and needed videos from all over the country of different news programmes and broadcasters.

In March 1999 Peter proposed. Jeremy was furious. The first day Sarah wore her engagement ring on air he spotted it. He immediately wrote her an angry letter demanding to know if the ring on her engagement finger meant that she had got engaged or was it 'some other kind of ring'. Jeremy felt that their 'relationship' was compromised. How could he stalk someone who was going to get married and one day have somebody else's children?

He sent a card to congratulate her but commented that he'd be happy if Peter died or disappeared.

> 'This is the last thing you will receive from me for a couple of weeks, honest. ... I hope you're happy, I suppose, even if I would enjoy it if your fiancée died by falling into some acid or getting eaten alive by maggots. Think of these words and think of me feeling sad. For nearly one year I have loved every inch of you. But from today I will always hate one of your fingers, the finger that holds your ring.'

Despite Jeremy's fury he seemed to get over the change in the 'relationship'. Even the knowledge that Sarah was engaged to Peter and that they were going to get married didn't stop him. If anything, in common with many other stalkers, it seemed to make him even more obsessed and heightened his sense of anticipation. He was almost saying, 'It's temporary, you'll get over it and finally come to your senses'.

A new incident gave Sarah the biggest fright she'd had so far. She arrived home to discover a letter had arrived – from Jeremy. Sarah was terrified. She thought Jeremy had finally found out her home address. Luckily the incident was a false alarm. The letter had been re-routed from her former university in Bristol. This was a relief in one sense but it was also a reminder that Jeremy was prepared to go to any length to track her down.

The murder of Jill Dando on the morning of Monday, April 26, changed everything. The death of the popular television presenter caused a huge public reaction of horror and anger. It also put the television industry on alert. BBC security was stepped up after new threats were made against the presenter John Humphrys, and other BBC personnel. At Meridian, Lloyd Bracey and his colleagues were assessing their own situation. The investigating team's nationwide appeal for information about potential male stalkers was ringing alarm bells. The investigators were even more specifically requesting information on any men who had tried to contact female presenters over a continuous time period. Jeremy quickly came to mind.

His reaction to Dando's murder made him seem even more of a threat. Instead of expressing horror and anger, Jeremy was enjoying the moment. His writing indicated that he felt vindicated in some sense. He had done the right thing, stalking a female newsreader – it was clearly the fashionable thing to do. Sarah recalled the letters:

> 'He sent in some rather sick poems about Jill Dando and some sick comments. I think it fueled his whole fantasy about television presenters and serial killers.'

Jeremy felt Dando's murder gave him the opportunity to regain, what he believed to be, his central role in Sarah's life. For Sarah this was the most threatening part of Jeremy's attentions to date. He sent her notes commenting on how glad he was that a newsreader had been murdered but saying that he would have kidnapped her first. In one letter he said:

> 'You looked a bit miserable on the Monday Show. I suppose you would be considering Jill Dando just got her brains blown out by a probable stalker.'

Other comments were even more alarming:

'I have worked out a theory on why Jill Dando
was murdered. Jill rhymes with Kill. Dead
rhymes with head. She used to read news
bullet-ins. Simple when you have the right
kind of mind. Kill Jill dead, with a bullet
through the head.'

Jeremy inserted Jill Dando's name into poems and
sent them to Sarah, 'Jack and Jill went up the hill to fetch
a pail of water. Jack fell down and broke his crown and
Jill – got shot by a stalker'. At no time did he express any
regret that Dando had been murdered.

By June 1999, the Jill Dando investigation was into its
second month. The detectives were following a variety of
different and unconnected leads. After much investigating
and interviewing they were coming to the conclusion that
a lone gunman had shot Jill Dando. The man was most
likely obsessive and may have been stalking the presenter
for some time. As a fellow stalker, Jeremy was basking in
the reflected "glory", '...I have just heard on the radio
that police believe the gun in the Jill Dando murder was
purchased in a Midlands pub. Oh no! The police are
onto me....' Jeremy must have known that his behaviour
would eventually attract the interest of the police. He
still believed however that he was a 'good' stalker and
continued to tell Sarah that she was lucky to have him:

'... even though I write you letters and send
you presents etc. you can never afford to take
me for granted. Ultimately you are dependent
on my maintaining goodwill towards you.
There is no reason why I should lose this
though. It is for you to make sure you do not
upset me as I have no intention of upsetting

you. Even though we may be stalker/victim, I
like to think you are happy enough with me
and that you can enjoy being stalked a bit.'

Jeremy set out his own take on the Dando murder.
According to his letter he would have approached the
matter in an altogether different way.

'If I was stalking Jill Dando I'd have kidnapped
her or done something else to her rather than
shooting her in the head. How can you shoot
someone in the head – unless you hate them
of course? It seems a waste of a victim if you
ask me. He could have used her before killing
her eg, by raping or assaulting her, getting his
money's worth as it were. This is as honest as
I can be Sarah. Telling it as I see it.'

Sarah felt that this was the last straw. She remembers
that '…it was chilling – because I was in the same position
as Jill Dando, I was a news presenter and what was he
planning for me?' Sarah agreed with her management
colleagues that the time had come to notify the police.
Jeremy's persistence, and his new obsession with com-
paring his treatment of Sarah to his hypothetical, copycat
treatment of Jill Dando, convinced everyone at Meridian
that Jeremy Dyer had the potential to be dangerous. At
the very least, he was someone who should be investigated
further.

There is a certainly a question mark over the delay in
deciding to inform the police about the behaviour of Jeremy
Dyer and the serious nature of the letters he had been
sending. In reading the letters as they are detailed above,
one could be forgiven for thinking that the entire Meridian

newsroom waited around for the post to arrive every day to see what Jeremy would have to say in his latest missive. This couldn't be further from the reality of the situation. Meridian is a busy place and Jeremy's activities were just another in a series of ongoing difficulties which beset a busy newsroom on a daily basis. The truth is that Sarah and her colleagues kept a close eye on Jeremy's letters but they had felt right from the start that he was a harmless freak, someone who was more likely to 'bark' than 'bite'.

The death of Jill Dando acted as a wake up call. In late May 1999, Sarah and Lloyd finally contacted the police and showed them the eighty or so letters which had arrived from Jeremy. The police were shocked. According to Sarah they actually 'blanched'. It was at this point that Sarah herself thought 'What Have I been playing with here?' Compared with the response of, for example, Jodie Foster to the very strange letters she had received from her stalker John Hinckley, Sarah's reactions were somewhat lackadaisical. Dyer had been given free rein for some time and the lack of intervention had certainly spurred him on to become more adventurous in his writings and suggestions.

The detectives, led by Neil Parker, were given the bundles of correspondence to take away as evidence. It took the police almost two days to wade through all the letters. Some of the more serious letters contained references to murders, detailing the horrific ways some people were killed. Jeremy had also searched the Internet for references to other stalkers. Neil Parker commented:

> 'It concerned me that Jeremy might take the fixation to the next level and actually attempt to meet Sarah in person and that he might do something to harm Sarah.'

They sent Jeremy's details to the Dando enquiry before deciding what to do about his potential threat to Sarah. They decided to track him down for questioning.

Neil Parker went to Coventry on June 11, 1999 and found Jeremy without any difficulty. After all, months before he had given Sarah his full name and address. He had done nothing since to hide the details of his life at the University of Warwick. He was even working in a local school as part of his teacher-training course. It was at the school that Neil Parker finally met Jeremy and explained why he was there. He arrested Jeremy and took him back to Kent for questioning.

While Jeremy's arrest didn't appear to be any surprise to him – he may even have enjoyed it, after all he was now a fully-fledged stalker – the incident came as a complete shock to his family. The Dyers are a respectable family; Jeremy's aunt is a magistrate and no one in the family had ever found themselves on the wrong side of the law. A search of Jeremy's room in Coventry had revealed law books marked at pages detailing stalking legislation. He had obviously studied the law in relation to prosecution for crimes of harassment in detail. Parker felt that Jeremy believed the books would help him to beat any possible charge the police could lay against him.

Jeremy was charged with harassment under section 4 of the Protection from Harassment Act and with the more serious charge of making threats to kill. He was remanded to HM Prison Elmley at Sheerness on the Isle of Sheppey, which is located on the north coast of Kent.

The trial of Jeremy Dyer began in December 1999. Sarah knew that meeting her stalker face-to-face was going to be a very difficult moment. She remembers driving to the trial feeling like she was going to meet her 'Nemesis'. It was a terrible experience. By making her appear in a court to prosecute someone who believed that he was having a relationship with her meant, Sarah felt, that Jeremy had already achieved the upper hand. Throughout the proceedings, she felt like the one who was being accused.

Neil Parker and the other detectives commented that the trial appeared to be the culmination of Jeremy's efforts over the past eighteen months to get close to Sarah. During the trial Jeremy got to see Sarah in the flesh everyday, practically face-to-face. Parker noticed Jeremy's continued obsession. When Sarah gave evidence Parker felt Jeremy was 'fixated on her' and that he 'continuously looked at her'. Sarah's job was to appear in front of hundreds of thousands of viewers every night of the week but she found her courtroom appearance an infinitely more daunting experience. Naturally she wasn't worried about appearing in public. Her fears and nervous reaction were a direct result of having to meet Jeremy.

> 'I was very nervous with my heart beating out of my chest and I had to get through it … It wasn't really fair that I was the one who had to meet him. He got what he wanted because he got to spend half a day in court drinking in my presence, just a few yards from me, looking at me and being in my company – which is not what I wanted at all.'

In his evidence Jeremy said that he wasn't stalking Sarah. She knew who and what he was. He didn't believe that he was doing her any harm. Neil Parker refutes this claim. As he points out you can't send somebody over eighty letters and make detailed references to assault and violence without making them fear for their safety. The physical evidence of the letters, cards and presents were supported by detailed psychiatric evidence.

The psychiatric evidence clearly demonstrated Jeremy's deteriorated mental condition. His obsessive behaviour had been generated by his poor social and emotional skills. They, in turn, had increased his narcissism, encouraging a belief in his own intellectual and sexual prowess. His lack of friends and social contact in general meant that he had focused his attentions into 'projects'. He became so intensely involved in his 'projects' that he had room for nothing else in his life. His pursuit of Sarah Lockett was one such 'project'. It was concluded that Jeremy was happier to be involved in a mental relationship with a fantasy person than actually be involved in a real relationship. It was also concluded that Jeremy was harmless in general but there was a question mark over his intentions towards Sarah. On the subject of the letters the Crown prosecutor suggested that they were certainly intended to make her feel that violence would be used against her.

During the trial Jeremy changed his plea to guilty and admitted the crime of harassment. However, he continued to plead his innocence in relation to any threats to kill Sarah. The changed plea meant that the jury could only reach a verdict on the threats to kill charge but they were unable to reach one. The judge directed them to return a verdict of not guilty. He then sentenced Jeremy to two and a half years imprisonment for harassment. In her ruling, the trial judge described Jeremy as an 'extremely weird' young man. Judge Susan Hamilton commented:

> 'It was impossible for Ms Lockett to tell if Dyer was a timid individual or a mad axe murderer.'

Jeremy was taken back to HM Prison Elmley in January 2000 to serve his sentence.

According to Sarah, the whole experience, although frightening and threatening for her, has yielded some positives. She feels:

> 'It gave a good signal to other stalkers that you can't muck about with television presenters. They're not public property to be threatened in this way … I suppose he got his way in that he did get to meet me – but he did get a prison sentence.'

After serving fifteen months of his two-year sentence, Jeremy was released from prison. Sarah felt threatened and was extremely worried that Jeremy would come to her house when he got out. Although Jeremy will go back to prison if he ever contacts Sarah again she still feels the need to check the street outside her house everyday just to make sure that there is nobody there. Faced with the question of what did Jeremy Dyer want with a woman he knew he couldn't have? Sarah replied,

> 'I think at first he wanted to go out with me on a date… be my boyfriend… that sort of thing. They said at the trial "Why did you pick Sarah? Why did you stalk Sarah?". He said, "it's very personal; it's like falling in love".'

For Sarah Lockett, Jeremy Dyer will always be an unwelcome part of her life. What began as simple fan mail intensified to such a degree that colleagues, and eventually the police, feared that the escalation of Jeremy's obsession and its increasingly threatening nature, could lead to a tragic outcome. Jeremy, perhaps deliberately, created a situation where he left Sarah and the police with no option but to act decisively. In many ways, the trial achieved Jeremy's ultimate stalking fantasy. Jeremy the stalker had successfully engineered a situation where he would now be part of his victim's life forever and Sarah would never forget him. As Sarah commented:

> 'He and I will always be bound together – in the press cuttings, in the fact that we were in that trial together. I don't want to be bound to him, but I am, and he's bound to me and maybe that's made him feel close to me and he's achieved what he wanted.'

CHAPTER SIX

Revenge

Expert observers have devised different categories to describe different types of stalkers. A potential stalker's personality can have a variety of characteristics that fall into a mixture of these categories. In cases of 'simple obsession', a stalker or obsessed person has usually had a previous relationship with the person they pursue. But just because 'simple obsession' is a stalker's main motivation this doesn't mean that he or she cannot also have stalking tendencies involving an erotomania obsession.

Andrew Cunanan came from a dysfunctional American family. His mother, MaryAnn Schillaci, of Sicilian parentage, met Modesto 'Pete' Cunanan, a native Filipino in a bar in Long Beach in 1961. He had joined the US Navy ten years previously on his arrival from the Philippines. Pete was a 'corpsman' who worked in navy hospitals but was anxious to improve his position. He was acutely conscious of his Filipino background. Although she was engaged back in Ohio, MaryAnn was immediately impressed by Pete who was ten years her senior. They began a passionate affair and got married in May 1961, when MaryAnn was six months pregnant.

Navy life meant a variety of postings for Pete while MaryAnn remained in California. By the time they moved to National City, a small shipbuilding town on the outskirts of San Diego, the couple had three children, Christopher, Elena and Regina. The lengthy separations continued and fuelled suspicion between them. At one point Pete believed that he was not the father of one of their children. By all accounts the marriage was not a happy one and there were rumours of physical and verbal abuse. Pete, who had been transferred to the Fleet Marines as the Vietnam War intensified, was working in the Naval Hospital in San Diego when Andrew was born in 1969. The relationship between MaryAnn and Pete, fractious at the best of times, took a turn for the worse as MaryAnn succumbed to a serious case of post-natal depression, the first of many recurring depressions she would suffer.

In 1972 Pete retired from the Navy with his full pension entitlements as a Chief Petty Officer. He dreamt of a new career in financial services and began a course of study which eventually led to an MBA. A year after Pete's retirement the family moved a few miles away to 5777 Watercrest Drive, in the suburb of Bonita. Using money inherited from MaryAnn's father, the Cunanans bought a California 'Ranch' style house in this middle-class suburb. With the new house came proximity to better schools and a more refined class of neighbour.

Andrew, however, didn't want to mix with the neighbours. He believed he was different and deserved more. Certainly in his neighbourhood, where the children of emigrant families generally ended up in manual labour jobs, he *was* different. Three things meant that he stood out from the crowd. He was very good looking, with dark eyes and the 'all year tan' skin tone usually found in children from Filipino/European parentage. He also appeared to be very bright. He memorised huge sections of the encyclopaedia and had supposedly, perhaps at his religious mother's urging, read the bible by the time he was seven. The third and most distinctive thing about him was his apparent inability, or possibly disinclination,

to socialise with children of his own age. While the other
boys were out playing baseball or simple games during
the summer months, Andrew was indoors reading his
encyclopaedia or watching television. Described as 'a
typical Mama's boy', Andrew clung to his mother and
she was highly possessive and defensive of him. It is clear
that his relationship with his father was somewhat similar,
although less intense. Vying for Andrew's affection or
approval, even when he was a small boy, seems to have
been an ongoing source of competition between MaryAnn
and Pete – as the youngest he was their favourite child.
Whereas his mother would smoother him with affection,
Pete took Andrew on trips around town. They would
often buy new clothes, usually for Andrew. Pete imbued
in his son a sense of doing better for himself – wearing
the right clothes, looking good, getting noticed. For
Andrew this code of beliefs were high on his scale of
values from an early age.

As a result of his parents' favouritism Andrew was
allowed to do exactly what he wanted. His intelligence,
good looks and newly acquired style, added to his self-
importance, even at this early age. His parents enrolled
him at the nearby Bonita Vista Junior High School.
Twelve-year-old Andrew entered the school with an
exceptional IQ of 147. He spent two years at Bonita,
years in which his personality and image bore little
resemblance to his real roots. His adoring but increasingly
estranged parents did not discourage this change. To
observers he was trying to turn himself into a sophisticate.

By 1982, aged thirteen, Andrew was re-inventing
himself. He attempted to portray himself as the pampered
son of a rich family. Even at this early stage in his life he
blatantly lied about his roots. Andrew never referred to
the fact that he was half-Filipino and never mixed with

his Filipino classmates. Other students noted his attempts at superiority and the fact that he spoke of stocks and shares and restaurants and clothes. Apparently he once complained at a classmate's twelfth birthday party that there was no *Perrier* to drink! Most people viewed Andrew's 'posing' as the eccentricities of an impressionable young boy. It was easy to believe that his pretensions would soon be ironed out by High School or by the harsh realities of the real world.

The next year he was accepted by the exclusive Bishops School at La Jolla. A west-coast version of an Ivy League prep school, Bishops was the epitome of social acceptance for Andrew and his family. MaryAnn had sent applications to a number of private schools in the area and Bishops was certainly the best one – where the money would come from was another question. The basic tuition fees were around $5,000 per annum. MaryAnn and Pete decided that it was worth it.

They seemed happy to participate in the fantasy, however temporary, of Andrew as a bright, rich boy entering a school he deserved to be in by birthright. It is difficult to assess the effect Andrew's special treatment had on his siblings. The two older children, Christopher and Elena, were pretty much left to their own devices and were described by their mother as 'street kids'. The younger daughter, Gina, was intelligent like Andrew and appeared to have also benefited from some of the more privileged treatment he received.

Andrew's handwritten application form for Bishops certainly illustrated his desire to be somebody different. It was also an indication of his innate ability to embellish his circumstances. When asked what he did with, 'Time to do as you please', Andrew claimed that he was 'a fanatical reader' and also enjoyed 'chess, clothes, *Mercedes* and running'. He stated that his one wish would be to have 'success, a house overlooking the ocean, two *Mercedes*, four beutiful [sic] children, three beutiful [sic] dogs and a good relationship with God'.

The fact that these applications were made under the supervision of his mother tells its own tale. The mother-son relationship was as intense as ever and Andrew had manipulated both his parents into doing exactly what he wanted.

At Bishops, Andrew adopted a new, outwardly rich and confident persona. He denied any Filipino roots and spoke little about his family. Despite having positioned himself on the launch pad for his future success, way above the level one would have expected from a child with Andrew's background, he felt very resentful. Most of his classmates were actually well-off and were born into the social whirl for which Bishops prepared them. The school liked to portray the image that it was an egalitarian outfit where all students were equal – developing knowledge of the poorer sections of society and their circumstances was considered a positive educational tool. However, getting to know the poor and being one of them are two entirely different things.

Andrew was careful not to risk social ostracism by being true to his roots. Here was an opportunity to get ahead, to leave the no-hope deprivation of his National City beginnings behind and become 'someone' – what's more, his parents shared his vision and were willing to play along with whatever it took to help Andrew to get ahead.

Andrew's flamboyance began to get him noticed by the other students. There was no doubt that his unusual dress styles and effeminate manner singled him out among the other boys – no big surprise here, Andrew had always wanted to stand out. According to Maureen Orth in her book *Vulgar Favors*:

> 'the twenties and thirties in France and England were favourite points of reference, particularly because Andrew thought of them as "gay eras".... He was so enthralled by Evelyn Waugh's novel *Brideshead Revisited*, that ... In emulation of Flyte, Andrew started carrying a teddy bear he named Bully around Bishops.'

Still under the influence of his protective mother, Andrew avoided female company and gravitated towards the less threatening male members of his class. Andrew's effeminate, and often outrageous, behaviour certainly got him noticed but, surprisingly, he remained relatively untouched by potential bullies. Andrew's behaviour was so outrageously camp and overtly effeminate that they just ignored him. Certainly any boy brave enough to effectively announce, "I am gay' in his early teens in Andrew's fashion, would be looked upon as someone possessing exceptional courage or exceptional stupidity – among Andrew's male peers it just led to confusion. Maureen Orth writes:

> 'Andrew quickly realised that playing the flaming fag got him the renown he was so desperate for. When anyone called him a sissy, Andrew, would rejoin with lightning speed "you want some?".

According to Orth, Andrew's classmates were divided on his behaviour. Many liked him, finding him ' suave, generous and genuinely concerned for people', others thought he was 'sad and pathetic'. As the years went by some fellow students felt that Andrew 'just got progressively worse – louder and more exaggerated – you could hear him halfway down the hallway and he was fun to be around, just as a train wreck or a streaker is fun to be around – it's outrageous, it's a mess, and it's fun to watch!'

At what point Andrew moved from being a camp attention grabber to becoming a fully-fledged, practicing homosexual is unknown. By the time he was leaving Bishops he had certainly experimented and had made contacts in the gay world of Southern California. There's certainly evidence that by aged fifteen he was already a well-known figure in some of San Diego's gay bars. He boasted to anyone who would listen of his torrid, sexual encounters with older gay men who gave him presents and money for sex. His stories revolted some and titillated others – whether they were true or it was the usual Andrew attention grabbing bravado style lies, no one was ever sure.

Pete had given Andrew a *Mastercard*. This gave him the chance to impress his circle of friends by hosting free dinners. He often called himself Andrew DeSilva when booking a table. The DeSilvas, a rich family who lived in a small area of multi-million dollar homes north of La Jolla, personified what Andrew aspired to be – wealthy beyond belief, connected and sophisticated. Andrew certainly used the DeSilva name in the gay bars where he had begun to hang out late into the night.

The *Mastercard* soon proved useless however. On the Cunanan domestic front the friction between Pete and MaryAnn finally ended in a bust-up in 1988. The separation didn't follow any formal break-up – Pete just disappeared; one day he was gone, leaving MaryAnn and the family with nothing. He even sold the heavily mortgaged house and his car. A long run of 'bad luck' at his broking job had finally caught up with him. He disappeared in a cloud of suspicion and financial allegations, using a holiday visa to return to his native Philippines.

Despite having had a closer relationship with his mother, Andrew was devastated when he realised that Pete had left. It also presented him with another difficulty. Even though he'd managed to keep Pete out of the picture to a large extent how would he explain his departure to his well-heeled classmates? Plus Pete's disappearance caused a major funding crisis. Now in his last year at Bishops, Andrew realised that the money would not be there to get him into one of the top colleges which his classmates would be attending.

At the end of his final High School year Andrew was almost back where he had started – on the bottom rung of the ladder – with no Ivy League college to go to and a home life in ruins. What he did have, however, was a series of contacts from Bishops and a highly refined ability to lie and invent prestige-building stories and personas. At the end of the term he appeared in the Bishops' yearbook as the student 'most likely to be remembered'. It may have been a genuine observation by his classmates or a backhanded compliment – little did the other students realise how 'remembered' Andrew Cunanan would become.

Andrew enrolled as a history student at La Jolla College in the University of California, San Diego. He soon moved out of the Cunanan household. Leaving home most probably coincided with the emergence of the real Andrew Cunanan – but who was he? From this point on 'Andrew Cunanan' became a series of imaginary people, people

Andrew had always wanted to be. Away from his family he could be whom he liked and do whatever he wanted. Friendships with rich young people had opened new doors for Andrew. His imagination, his desire to get on and achieve his goals, and his ruthless narcissistic streak were finally being given opportunities to breathe.

Just after he graduated and before he could fully embark on his new life Andrew decided he needed to travel to the Philippines to see his father. He was horrified by what Pete had done to his mother and was confused by his sudden departure. His father's situation in Manila horrified him even further. Pete was living in a shack in one of the poorest parts of Manila; Open sewers spilled onto the streets, chickens and pigs shared rooms with humans and a smell of decay lingered everywhere. Andrew is reported to have comforted himself somewhat by trawling the gay red light district of the sprawling city – whether he was a buyer or a seller is unclear. His original mission may have been to confront or to forgive Pete – he hardly stayed long enough to give either a chance. He left after just five days.

Back in California Andrew was offered a dream arrangement. Liz Cote, a friend from Bishops, was about to be married to Philip Merrill, ten years her senior. The couple were planning to live at Berkeley in San Francisco. Liz was rich and sociable and had taken to Andrew because she found him amusing. Philip liked him too and felt it would be good for her to have a friend around, particularly one as sexually unthreatening as Andrew. To be a constant companion and live in opulent surroundings rent-free suited Andrew down to the ground. Berkeley was located just across the bay from Castro, an area of the city known as 'The crossroads of the gay world' – this proved a real bonus.

Andrew fitted in very well with Liz and Philip's lifestyle. He helped around the house and had the use of the car whenever he wanted. When they married in March 1989 he was the best man and became godfather to their first child in 1990. He got work as a temp at a number of large financial institutions in San Francisco. The filing and sorting jobs were hardly onerous, in fact they were somewhat insulting to a man of Andrew's intellect. But he didn't really want to work. Liz would have given him money if he had asked her but he didn't want to take it. Having his own money also gave him his independence, however limited. What money he did earn was poured into the bars and clubs of the Castro district.

Despite his outrageous antics at Bishops, which Liz had frequently witnessed, Andrew had never actually categorically said that he was gay. In fact Andrew had never owned up to being anyone. He lived a double live at Berkeley – by day he was Andrew Cunanan the sociable, helpful house-sitter and sometimes temporary worker; by night he was a dedicated cruising homosexual with a penchant for the dark side of San Francisco's gay scene. The range of Andrew's sexual contacts cannot be enumerated directly by counting the men who say they knew him, or had sexual contact with him, at the time. As a compulsive liar, lying about who he was, where he came from, and his social and financial circumstances, the number of relationships he may have had in his different persona are difficult to quantify. As plain Andrew Cunanan he had many relationships. As Andrew DeSilva, which was certainly an alias he still frequently used, he had many other encounters.

Andrew also used the name Drew Cummings as an alias. In his 'Drew' persona he would tell prospective targets tales of his adventures as a navy lieutenant. The

Castro district caters for all homosexual preferences. Late night bars and clubs such as the *Midnight Sun* and *Badlands* were favourite spots for pick-ups and short term, no questions asked, intercourse. Andrew would leave the Merrills home with little money and return with plenty of change in his pocket. He'd describe the dinner and drinks he had consumed – there was never any mention of where the money came from.

At the *Midnight Sun* Andrew met Eli Gould, a Jewish attorney heavily involved in representing clients in the burgeoning software industry based in and around San Francisco. Within weeks Andrew was saying he was half-Jewish, a bizarre claim for someone so obviously of Filipino extraction. But this was Andrew's 'flavour of the month' and like all short-term fads, he played it to the maximum. Eli became one of Andrew's buddies. His connections were yet another potential door opener for the socially hungry Cunanan. It is at this point that Andrew had his now infamous encounter with Gianni Versace.

Versace was born in Reggio Calabria, at the southernmost tip of the Italian mainland on December 2, 1946. Fascinated with fashion and design in all forms and anxious to escape from the sometimes conservative and restrictive environment of the Italian south, he moved to Milan at the age of twenty-five to work as a fashion designer.

By fashion standards, his rise was meteoric. He presented his first collection for women signed with his own name in a fashion show at the Palazzo della Permanente, in Milan in 1978. International recognition quickly followed. In 1982 he won the first of a series of the awards which would become characteristic of his meteoric career, 'L'Occhio d'Oro' for the best fashion designer of the 1982/83 Autumn/Winter collection for women. The collection displayed the famous metal garments, which became a classic feature of his fashion style. The same year, he began to collaborate with the Teatro alla Scala and designed costumes for the Richard Strauss ballet *Josephlegende*.

By the mid-eighties the Versace fashion house had grown beyond clothes by launching fragrances, accessories, furniture and anything else that could be considered 'fashionable' into the worldwide market. His interest in theatre and ballet continued; he won acclaim all over Europe for his designs for both Art forms. His network of shops and design Emporia also continued to grow apace. Branches were opened in most major European capitals. By 1989 the Versace Empire had become a multi-million dollar enterprise. While unwilling to flaunt his homosexuality, Gianni never hid it, and became very involved in AIDS related charities, along with his friends Elton John and Princess Diana. To the gay world he was an icon at a level above any other gay icon. In the homosexual community to meet Versace was more than just a happening, it was a badge of honour, a life-changing event.

There appears to be no doubt that Andrew did meet Gianni Versace. What is less clear, however, is the level to which the relationship was alleged to have grown. The claims are wide and varied – needless to say the more extravagant claims were made by Andrew himself – but there are witness testimonies from reliable sources to underpin stories that Andrew's dealings with one of the world's most famous fashion designers were more than just a friendly handshake.

As Maureen Orth relates in *Vulgar Favors*, Versace had designed costumes for the San Francisco Opera's production of Richard Strauss's *Capriccio* which opened in October 1990. The arrival of a serious gay icon into the midst of the San Francisco gay community was a major news story. There was intense competition for tickets and for invitations to any other related social engagements. One of these was a party at the Colossus, a huge gay disco, that Versace had planned to attend as part of his introduction to the San Francisco gay scene. Val Caniparoli, a choreographer with the city's ballet gave VIP passes to Eli Gould – Eli invited Andrew. According to Orth, when it became known that Val would be working with Versace, Andrew commented, 'I know him. I've met him before'. He claimed that he'd met Versace in his home country, Italy. Andrew, of course, had never been to Italy. The only evidence, often quoted, which some believe demonstrated that Andrew *did* actually know Versace, is what happened at the Colossus that night.

Andrew and Eli awaited the arrival of the great man in the VIP room of the Colossus club. Versace swept in with his entourage and stood centre stage, as the devoted and the curious paid their respects. Suddenly Versace walked over to Andrew and apparently said, 'I know you, Lago di Como, no?'. His house on the Swiss border was reputedly often a subject he used to open up conversations. By all accounts Andrew was thrilled and replied, 'That's right, thanks for remembering, Signor Versace'. Andrew then introduced Eli to Versace and the three spoke for a while before the designer moved off.

Other alleged sightings of Andrew with or near Versace during the few days he remained in San Francisco have fuelled the rumour that the two were more than passing acquaintances. As Maureen Orth states, Doug Stubblefield, another Cunanan friend, claimed to have seen Andrew sitting with the designer in Versace's white limousine. LA lawyer Eric Gruenwald also remembered seeing

Andrew with Versace at the Colossus. Whatever the substance of these stories there is no doubt that the experience of finally meeting someone he regarded as 'royalty' had had an effect on Andrew. He had basked in reflected glory when the fashion icon singled him out for special treatment. Andrew wanted more similar experiences.

Many of the rumours which allege other encounters between Andrew and Versace can be completely discounted; But there are some which have enough in the way of truth and eye-witness testimony to be, at least, semi-believable. The problem of establishing whether or not they are true lies with Andrew himself. His propensity to exaggerate and lie led to the suspicion that any further references to nights out, or even sexual encounters, with Versace were figments of his fertile imagination, designed to attract the excited attention of fawning young men. However, chasing Versace, in whatever form it might take, would have to wait. There were more pressing problems to be dealt with.

Andrew's life changed again – the Merrills had decided to move to Sacramento. Andrew felt that Sacramento would be no place for him. But life without the Merrills meant a significant financial downgrade and without the comfort zone of understanding and financially secure housemates. Instead of facing the realities of San Francisco without Liz and Phil, Andrew reverted to type, moving back to live with his mother and re-enrolling in UCSD. He began to hang around a more affluent gay set – the Hillcrest set – rich older men with a penchant for pretty, younger boylike twenty somethings. In this predominantly gay area of San Diego, Andrew became a well-known figure around the bars. He certainly created difficulties for himself by trying to cultivate relationships with the older, more discreetly gay, men while still indiscriminately cruising the late night bars. If they were going to take an interest in Andrew then they didn't want the world to know about it.

In 1992, Andrew met one of the men who would feature prominently in his life. Jeff Trail was a handsome, young navy officer from DeKalb, Illinois. He came from an all-American conservative mid-west family with a military tradition. Jeff won a place at the United States Navy Academy at Annapolis, Maryland. He was homosexual but had, up until now, remained firmly in the closet. When Jeff's ship docked at San Diego he was attracted to Hillcrest and, in turn, to Andrew. Jeff was good looking, good company and, on the surface, straight – in a military sort of way. The infatuated Andrew wanted their affair to become a grander romance but Jeff was more interested in the other young men Andrew introduced him to. It's clear that once Jeff accepted the fact that he was gay, he got into the scene in a fairly serious way. His popularity inevitably led to a string of short-term romances. Just as inevitably, Andrew was extremely jealous. While at first they socialised together, Jeff made other friends, in both the gay and straight communities. He was friendly, outgoing and likeable. In time these qualities would be the catalyst for Andrew Cunanan's killing spree and his determined stalking behaviour.

Around the time that Jeff was meeting other people, Andrew became involved with a much older man. Fifty-eight year old Norman Blachford was a soft-spoken multi-millionaire from Phoenix, Arizona, who holidayed at La Jolla. Older men were not necessarily Andrew's type but in Norman Andrew saw a meal ticket where he could call all the shots. Slow at first to part with his cash, Norman was soon entertaining Andrew at his home in

Phoenix or at La Jolla. They began to travel together. Andrew's knowledge of art, music and architecture, added to his intimate familiarity with the gay scene, captivated the older man who was less confident with his sexuality. Andrew became his almost constant companion and in 1995 he moved into Norman's condominium at La Jolla. He had the run of the place and the added bonus of being a 'kept man'. Norman paid for everything – credit cards, a new car, all Andrew's expenses. Their relationship certainly became the talk of the local gay scene. People started saying that Andrew had started a relationship with an affluent 'sugar daddy'.

Despite the material attractions, Andrew found Norman a bit of a strain. He kept in touch with Jeff, not out of friendship but in a manner which left Jeff in no doubt that Andrew still considered him 'his property'. While not always having to look over his shoulder, Jeff was aware of the need to humour Andrew. He'd seen his mood swings and knew that an Andrew "scorned" was something he did not necessarily want to have to deal with.

In November 1995, Andrew went on a visit to San Francisco, staying at the opulent Mandarin Oriental Hotel. He'd taken to travelling there, using Norman's money, to visit friends and to check out his old haunts in the Castro area. One evening he met David Madson. David had spent most of his life in the Minneapolis area before graduating from architecture school at the University of Minnesota. His homosexuality had remained under wraps for most of his young adult life. Like a lot of mid-western small-towners, he used his travels as opportunities to experiment in gay scenes. David thought Andrew was interesting, fun and knew his way around the Castro. Andrew considered David attractive, kind and thoughtful.

David's love and knowledge of all things architectural appealed to Andrew – and he was cute! The two hit it off immediately and spent their first night together at the Mandarin. Andrew decided not to tell David about his relationship with Norman. He promised to stay in contact with David when they parted.

Andrew, as usual, had lied to both men. Norman believed that Andrew was in San Francisco seeing his ex-wife and daughter, a cover he used for his frequent sex-driven trips to the bay area. David believed Andrew was a member of a wealthy family whose privacy demanded a low profile and secret address. Hence, it was up to Andrew to stay in touch and make the arrangements for them to see each other. Regular trysts were arranged for San Francisco while Andrew continued to live with Norman Blachford. At the same time Andrew still frequented the gay bars of San Diego and became somewhat involved in the S&M scene. But he was careful. He was a well-known figure in the San Diego gay area and preferred to indulge in this other facet of his multiple personalities on his travels.

Over the course of the next few months David and Andrew saw each other in Minneapolis and in San Francisco. Andrew had confided to his friends that he was 'in love' with David. By June 1996, Andrew had two successful relationships on the go (no mean feat for him) and both were producing their own rewards. In Norman he had an undemanding financier who provided him with an entrée into the social level he craved and who apparently wanted nothing more than company in return. In David he had a convenient, attractive lover, who seemed happy for him to call the shots. Alongside all of this he was able to live an entirely separate existence as a cruising homosexual in the gay bars and clubs where he had thrived for many years.

Later that month Norman entertained Andrew and Larry Chrysler, another of Norman's older friends, to a summer vacation at a villa in St Jean-Cap-Ferrat on France's Cote D'Azur. Located close to the city of Nice, Cap Ferrat is one of the most exclusive and expensive parts of the South of France; Regular visitors include Madonna and Elton John. Andrew had told David that he was visiting family at his summer home and sent him a number of postcards. However the relationship with Norman was about to end.

In previous months Andrew had become more demanding. The compliant and co-operative Norman had put up with Andrew's financial demands but his patience was wearing thin. The straw that broke the camel's back was Andrew's demand for a new *Mercedes* SL convertible, valued at over $125,000. When Norman refused, Andrew left in a dramatic, high-camp departure. Efforts to patch things up and 'renegotiate' Andrew's 'deal' with Norman came to nothing. Norman still refused to budge on the car, offering instead to raise Andrew's allowance. Andrew wrote to his older companion claiming compensation for the time they had spent together. In an effort to distance himself from accusations that he was a 'kept' man, Andrew had constantly told friends that he had given up his family inheritance to be with Norman. The matter ended when Norman paid him $15,000 before leaving for a pre-arranged holiday. The easy days with Norman were over and, given the speed with which gossip about the matter travelled through Andrew's circle, he would have difficulty finding a replacement.

Problems had also arisen with David Madson. Unable to contact Andrew during his South of France sojourn, David had become frustrated. When Andrew failed to show up for the 4th of July holiday, that they had agreed to spend together, David made his own plans. He also made a decision that he would try to distance himself from Andrew. He knew that relationships of this sort could be problematic; so many gay men he had known were in conventional relationships or had to be discreet for work or family reasons. But Andrew was different – he was openly gay but he was still unwilling to have a relationship. At this stage David seemed to have realised that Andrew was also a show-off, a compulsive liar, and someone who had no problem making all his stories and experiences fit his current requirements.

With David temporarily unattainable Andrew turned to Jeff Trail. After another miserable couple of years in the Navy, Jeff had quit for a training course in the California Highway Patrol. He thought it would be a more relaxed and understanding environment. He was disappointed and had moved on. He had been briefly living with his sister in the town of Concord before he found a new job with a propane manufacturer in Minneapolis. This was good news for Andrew – both of the main men in his life, whom he had even managed to introduce to each other on one of his trips were now in the same city – Minnesota beckoned.

Calling David first, Andrew persuaded him that it would be good for both Jeff and David if he came to Minneapolis to visit. A short stay turned into a number of weeks, nearly driving Jeff to distraction. A longer stay at David's loft apartment followed with Andrew apparently ignoring the fact that both David and Jeff were now in new relationships. Both men came to dinners with Andrew and Jeff attended a party in David's loft. When David went skiing with his boyfriend, Andrew offered to house sit for him and to take care of his dog. David was happy to allow Andrew to stay but thought it somewhat bizarre – Andrew had protested deep affection for David yet was happy to mind his place while he went away with another man. But this, somewhat schizophrenic behaviour, was classic Andrew Cunanan – no matter how much reality was staring him in the face, he would turn or re-invent a situation to suit his own requirements.

Back in San Diego, Andrew had moved in with a gay couple Tom Eads and Erik Greenman, and their dog, on Robinson Street. Andrew still had no definite source of income but appeared to have no shortage of money. He would sleep late, walk the dog and just hang around. The $15,000 from Norman was the only traceable money he had received in some time. Rumours began to surface, not for the first time, that Andrew was involved in some sort of drug dealing or gay gigolo work. If he was, then it was with unknown clients or accomplices. The gay scenes in San Francisco certainly provided access to drugs but few in Andrew's circle of friends were hardened users. The more experienced dealers would have been very unwise to have the indiscreet and flamboyant Cunanan as their courier. Nevertheless, he was known to have easy access to narcotics and was certainly a user.

The last quarter of 1996 was a very low period in Andrew's life. He had put on weight and was using a drug, or drugs, of some sort. Many people noticed his dishevelled appearance over the Christmas holiday period.

By early 1997 he was a walking wreck, caring little for his appearance and behaving in a moody and irascible fashion. He revisited Minneapolis in January and once again barged in on the lives of David Madson and Jeff Trail. Both men had been involved in a series of relationships and were happily getting on with their own separate lives. A visit from Andrew was a major inconvenience and could turn into a major embarrassment. It is, however, a huge indictment of the two men that they didn't reject Andrew Cunanan. He did, after all, live in another city and could probably have been put off with a little insistence. But Andrew had a captivating personality and could change, chameleon like, to whatever the mood dictated. It was probably the afterglow of the better times, when Andrew was fun and interesting, that continually persuaded both men to give him another chance. The difficulties were also tempered somewhat by his ability to throw large amounts of cash about. He would spend thousands of his mysteriously acquired cash on trying to woo David back into his life.

Back in San Diego it continued to play on his mind – Jeff and David, the two men, the two lives, in the twin cities of Minneapolis-St Paul. Andrew couldn't seem to get away from his obsession that not only were the two loves of his life moving in the same circles but that they were now also together as a couple. This had no basis in fact but he convinced himself that the two men were lovers and that they had cut him out. In late April Andrew finally decided to find out for himself and booked a flight to Minneapolis.

David was at the airport when Andrew arrived and took him to his loft building. Andrew gave no information as to the length of his proposed visit. On the night of his arrival, Andrew had dinner with David and some of his friends at a downtown restaurant. Afterwards the two went to a local gay dance club, the Gay Nineties, because Andrew had said he wanted to dance.

Jeff Trail was out of town for most of the weekend. Aware of Andrew's imminent arrival he'd taken Jon Hackett, his current boyfriend, away for a couple of days to celebrate Jon's birthday. David and Andrew were seen

together again on the Saturday night, April 26. A number
of people who ran into the two that evening attested to
the fact that Andrew did not appear to be in very good
form and that David appeared 'on edge'. Somehow or
other Andrew managed to be at Jeff Trail's apartment on
Sunday morning, despite the fact that Jeff wasn't there
and clearly didn't want Andrew around. He took a
telephone message from one of Jeff's work colleagues and
made a number of telephone calls, including one to
Norman Blachford.

On the way back from their trip Jeff confided to Jon
that he needed to meet up with Andrew on some important
business. He said that he had arranged to meet Andrew
at a coffee shop. Jeff arranged to meet Jon later that
evening.

What happened next is unclear – what motivated it is
even less clear. Sometime between about 9.10pm and
9.45pm both Andrew and Jeff arrived at David's apartment.
A violent row erupted between Jeff and Andrew in the
course of which Andrew took a heavy claw hammer and
smashed Jeff's head to pieces, inflicting fatal blows and
damaging him beyond recognition. The final blows were
meted out in the hallway. Jeff's head smashed against the
hall door as he finally hit the ground, motionless and
near death.

What caused Andrew to lose his temper and turn so
viciously on one former lover in front of another ex-lover
is still unclear. The motivation may have been the
connection between the two men. Some theories suggested
that Andrew's deteriorating mental state had indeed led
him to convince himself beyond all reasonable doubt that
Jeff and David were having, or had had, an affair, despite
David's constant protestations to the contrary over the
weekend. Andrew may have confronted Jeff about the

matter before he hacked him to death in front of Madson. Hapless and helpless, it appears David did nothing to intervene. More curious is his willingness to be complicit in the incident and to go along from here with whatever Andrew suggested.

Whether Andrew threatened David with the same fate as Jeff we will never know but he undoubtedly had David under his control in some way. Rather than try to escape or to call the police, David now became involved in cleaning the crime scene.

Reconstructing the crime from later reports they seemed to have first taken care of Jeff's body. Jeff fell on an Oriental rug so they rolled his body up in the rug and dragged it to rest against the living room sofa. In this position the body's legs were sticking out so they covered them in an off-white Afghan rug. Due to the ferocity of the attack there was a lot of blood to clean up. The supposition is that they used cloth and paper towels to wipe the floor. Despite these efforts to eradicate their presence from the crime scene, two sets of bloody footprints – one barefoot, one shod – were left on the hardwood floor. They removed Jeff's watch, which had stopped at 9.55pm, and his navy ring. They threw them into a plastic bag along with a blood-soaked t-shirt, the hammer and towels. They left the bag under the table. They also left Jeff's pager on his corpse.

What was going through David Madson's mind is hard to imagine. For a rational and seemingly right thinking man to ignore what had just happened in his home is unfathomable. Andrew must have convinced him that he was now an accessory to a crime and would have to face the same consequences as himself. Witnesses report seeing both men, individually and together, on the morning and into the afternoon of Monday April 28, while Jeff Trail's battered and mutilated body lay rolled up in a rug in the loft.

Meanwhile, Jon Hackett had begun his search for Jeff. When Jeff failed to arrive home Jon became worried. David Madson's friends and work colleagues were also seriously concerned for his welfare. Madson was a popular and diligent work colleague and just not showing up for work was not his style. By 4pm on Monday afternoon two of David's friends told the building's caretaker that something was seriously wrong. They persuaded her to let them into the loft. They were horrified by what they found.

By the time the police had been called David's friends were beginning to come to terms with the stark fact that their friend was dead. Investigators assumed that the body in the rug was that of David Madson. It took some time to establish that this was not the case. Wishing to keep the crime scene intact, the forensic investigators didn't remove the body from the rug. It was only after examining the corpse's hair that they established that the body was not that of David Madson. Friends told the police of the man called Andrew who had stayed with David for the previous weekend. The second theory to emerge, therefore, was that it was Andrew's body in the rug and that David Madson had murdered him. It was some time before the police discovered the truth.

On the morning of April 30, the Wednesday, they finally took the blood-soaked body out of the carpet. Jeff's identification was kept in his wallet which Andrew and David had failed to remove. The police now finally knew the identity of the body in the rug.

The confusion and the delay had offered Andrew and David a window of opportunity. Some time on Monday, late morning or early afternoon, they had packed a few

things and left Minneapolis in David's red jeep. Just how
close they came to being caught is difficult to say. At least
one witness attested that he saw them together close to
the apartment building; Andrew was remonstrating with
David, the latter's eyes were heavily swollen as if he had
been crying. A number of people saw them in and around
the loft on the Monday morning. At this time David's
relatives, friends and work colleagues were concerned for
his safety and had started looking for him – it was certainly
a close call.

The police were by now actively pursuing David
Madson as a murder suspect. They knew about the
existence of Andrew but not a lot more. Friends of David
Madson and Jeff Trail were supplying new information
by the hour. The investigators had been able to trace the
Madson family and were still looking for information about
the mysterious Andrew DeSilva. By Saturday, May 3,
however they knew exactly who they were looking for
and why.

That morning two fishing enthusiasts, Scott Schmidt
and Kyle Hilken, were out looking for potential campsites
for a weekend trip. The area is about fifty miles north of
the twin cities of Minneapolis-St Paul, on a country lane
leading to the town of Duluth. As they approached the
edge of the lake they saw a fully-clothed body lying on its
back. They immediately called the police who, after cross-
referencing with Minneapolis colleagues, quickly
established from the description supplied that the body
was that of David Madson. He had been shot three times
with .40 calibre bullets from a handgun – once in the
right eye, once in the right cheek and once in the back.
Curiously, despite being together for at least three days,
Andrew and David had been seen by no one, there was
no record of them staying anywhere and no record of

them making any purchases.

Whatever confusion there had been about who did what to whom was now cleared up. The police issued an urgent all points bulletin for Andrew Phillip Cunanan AKA DeSilva. The murders sent shockwaves through the San Diego, San Francisco and Minneapolis gay communities. People who had know Andrew, and there were a lot of them, were terrified. The message was simple, Andrew had flipped, as some had always suspected he would, and was capable of anything. People in the gay community who knew Andrew were wondering if they were his next potential victim. This terror frustrated the police's best efforts to solicit new information. Andrew had made many friends and acquaintances. He'd also made just as many enemies, some of whom were afraid to stay in their own apartments for fear that he might visit. The most worrying thing was the lack of information. Andrew had killed and then just disappeared – rumours circulated that he was a master of disguise and could pop up unnoticed anywhere, anytime. It was also suggested that he had stashed away hundreds of thousands of dollars from drug dealing and payments for sexual favours, giving him the ability to move around effortlessly.

The truth was quite the opposite. Initial investigation of Andrew's financial records showed that he had reached a financial and cash crisis. His credit card records showed that he had run up over $20,000 on two cards and that his credit was now cancelled. They also discovered that he had sold the car Norman Blachford had given him for $15,000 in cash. Police knew that without credit cards Andrew' trail would be more difficult to trace. His lack of cash would probably also make him more desperate and reckless in his actions.

By Saturday afternoon Andrew was in Chicago. Illinois

borders Minnesota, but the journey by road from north Minneapolis-St Paul to Chicago would still take many hours. It's hard to believe that Andrew wasn't seen, particularly as he was still driving David's red jeep. Up to this point, his murderous actions could in some sense be explained by the curious love triangle that existed between Jeff Trail, David Madson and Andrew Cunanan – what happened next is inexplicable.

Seventy-two-year old Lee Miglin was a rich, respected and hard working property developer. His wife Marilyn is a successful figure on the US home shopping Network. The Miglin's home is an early 1900s townhouse located just north of the Chicago downtown area. Somehow Andrew Cunanan managed to end up there on the evening of May 3. Marilyn was on a business trip and Lee was alone in the house. Investigators later believed that Andrew approached the unfortunate Miglin, on what spurious pretence we will never know, and took him at gunpoint to his garage. There, Andrew bound Miglin's wrists and gagged his mouth before attacking him with a garden hand shears, stabbing him several times in the chest. He finished him off by slitting his throat with a hacksaw, blood spurting everywhere. Andrew then walked into the Miglin's house and helped himself to food from the refrigerator. He used the bath and spent the night in the house before calmly leaving the next morning in Lee Miglin's dark green, luxury *Lexus* saloon car.

It's clear that Andrew had made no effort to conceal his identity while in Chicago. The red jeep was subsequently found on Astor Street, less than a hundred metres from Miglin's house. Stealing the *Lexus* would inevitably link Andrew to the crime. The killer and the car were the subject of a widespread police hunt, not only in the Chicago metropolitan area but all over Illinois

and beyond. Andrew was quite obviously out of control.
In a sense he now had what he had always craved –
notoriety, albeit of the most macabre sort, but recognition
none the less. It's easy to picture Andrew driving David's
jeep from Minnesota to Illinois listening to radio reports
of his exploits and revelling in the perverted glory of his
brutal actions.

When the jeep was found it introduced a new dimension
to the mystery. Despite the two murders, the case was
still seen by many as a love triangle, largely confined to
the gay community. Miglin's murder introduced an older,
wealthier man into the equation. Was he linked to the gay
community or were the police now facing the fact that a
multiple killer was on the loose and anyone could be a
target? The murders were a national story and police
forces nationwide were looking for the fugitive Andrew
Cunanan. This must have heightened Andrew's sense of
importance. His elevation to the FBI's 'Ten Most Wanted
List' surely gave him a rush. Andrew was described as
'armed and dangerous' and someone who should be
'approached with caution'.

The fact that Andrew remained undetected is quite
unbelievable. He continued to drive the same highly
recognisable luxury car across North America for the next
few days. He even used the vehicle's car phone which the
FBI traced at one point to Western Pennsylvania. When
he heard about this on the radio, Andrew threw the phone
out the car window.

Realising that all the publicity demanded a change of
vehicle he was on the lookout for something less
conspicuous. At Finn's Point Cemetery in Pennsville, on
the border of New Jersey and Pennsylvania, Andrew
spotted a red 1995 Chevrolet pick-up truck and stopped.
He knocked on the door of the cemetery caretaker's house

where forty-five-year-old William Reese was taking a break. Reese, a former electrician, had given up his job to become the full-time caretaker of the historic Civil War graveyard, a job he carried out with dedication and pride. Andrew demanded the keys of the pick-up at gunpoint and Reese handed them over readily. Andrew then shot him at point blank range in the back of the head. The truck was seen driving out of the area just after 6pm. When Reese's wife, worried that he hadn't arrived home, called the police, their search revealed Andrew's latest random execution. The abandoned *Lexus* allowed the police to do a fast licence plate search. They immediately established the killer's identity. Andrew Cunanan's infamous National profile continued to grow unchecked.

Reese's murder confirmed that the police were not dealing with a homosexual revenge plot. The heterosexuality of Lee Miglin, which had been unfairly compromised in the media because of his alleged 'connection' to Andrew Cunanan was also confirmed. Rumours throughout the gay communities of Chicago and San Francisco had suggested that the seventy-two-year-old was Andrew's former lover and that he had been conducting closet relationships for years, using his marriage to Marilyn as a front. Bill Reese's murder and the link to the cars, which Andrew had scarcely bothered to conceal, clearly indicated that police were dealing with a psychotic and out of control killer. Andrew was on a rampage and was probably enjoying the thrill of it all.

From Pennsville, Andrew drove south on Interstate 95. This national freeway dissects the heart of the eastern United States, from Maine to Florida. Little is known about his journey south on I-95 but by Sunday May 11 Andrew was in Miami Beach, Florida. In just a couple of days he had covered an extraordinary distance. He had, to all intents and purposes, disappeared without trace. A fugitive from justice with four murders under his belt and the entire weight of the FBI on his tail could have picked any of the hundreds of places en route to 'disappear' or at least to hide until things had cooled down a bit. But Andrew wasn't hiding and he did nothing to lower his profile when he arrived in Miami.

The question as to whether he drove the 1200 miles from Upstate Pennsylvania to Florida to stalk Gianni Versace is difficult to answer. Versace's movements were not public knowledge. When Andrew arrived in Miami the designer was in Europe which suggests that Andrew didn't have a definite plan of action. More plausible is the theory that the rampantly gay lifestyle associated with the Miami suburb of South Beach attracted Andrew. As in San Diego, San Francisco and Minneapolis, he thrived in predominantly gay areas in which he could spin his outlandish stories and live through his aliases. Certainly an opportunity to put some clear blue water between himself and the murders of Trail, Madson, Miglin and Reese, would have been uppermost in his mind. If a chance came to kill again, then he would probably take it.

Gianni Versace had spent a significant amount of time in Miami. His hugely successful fashion empire meant onerous and time-consuming worldwide commitments. Versace was tired. His schedule was often overwhelming and, despite the efforts of his sister Donatella to reduce his workload, 1997 had brought even greater success and the consequent drain on his resources. Most injurious of all was the suspicion, believed by many to be true, that the designer was HIV positive, and had been living with the condition for four years. 'I want to quieten down my life and enjoy more my privacy', Versace said in a press interview. He knew his health was not as good as it could be. He was becoming irascible and difficult to deal with. He decided to go to the South Beach.

Along with his holiday villa at Lake Como, South Beach was Versace's favourite relaxation spot. It had all he needed – all year round weather, a hectic social life if required, and a degree of anonymity which the more fashionable areas of Paris or Milan did not allow him. Most of all it was a homosexual paradise where the designer could indulge himself if he felt like it. A spell in South Beach was something he felt would do him the world of good. He liked to relax there, stroll around, have coffee at his favourite coffee shops, watch the world go by. The Versace entourage arrived in Miami on July 12 and moved into the gated villa on Ocean Drive. The villa was a shrine to the designer. It was opulent, extravagant and excessive in every way.

Andrew, meanwhile, operating very much at the other end of the luxury scale, had checked into the Normandy Plaza Hotel on Collins Avenue and 69th Street, just north of South Beach. The hotel is reputed to have been a summer vacation stop for many movie stars in the 1930s and 40s but bears no reminder of the glamour of that era. In reality it is a long-stay facility and many 'residents' have spent years in the place. Andrew was given room 322, and after a couple nights, agreed a monthly rate with Miriam Hernandez, a Cuban woman who still runs the front desk.

What Andrew did with his time in South Beach is largely unknown but there is evidence that he didn't have much money and that he frequented a local pawn shop where he traded most of his more valuable belongings for cash. He did spend time in gay bars and clubs and appears to have blended effortlessly into the South Beach scene. They were unaware that a killer was in their midst. A month in the Miami area had certainly taken the steam out of the Andrew Cunanan story. While the FBI certainly had him at the top of their list, there was no tangible evidence to suggest that Andrew had headed as far south as Florida, nor was there any known reason for him to go there. Certainly those who knew him in his former haunts in California were on edge that an unstable Andrew might be on his way back home. Nobody imagined he'd travelled all the way to Florida – Andrew, it appeared, had fooled them all again.

In South Beach he'd all but disappeared out of sight. His arrival and departure times at the Normandy Plaza had become so erratic that it was impossible to know whether or not he was in or out of the hotel at any time. Where he spent his time is unclear. He was certainly low on finances, compared to more recent times and this lack of funds, something he was unaccustomed to, kept him out of the expensive gay haunts of South Beach. He was undoubtedly also conscious of his notoriety and the fact that he could be recognised at any time in connection with the recent killings. The most likely explanation for the lack of sightings of Andrew during this period is that he spent it stalking his victim. Andrew was in Miami for some time prior to the arrival of Versace on July 12 and had, almost certainly, inquired about the whereabouts of the designer. The ruthless manner in which he executed Versace indicated the seriousness with which Cunanan pursued him between his arrival and his death three days later.

The porter at the Normandy Plaza realised on the Saturday morning that Andrew had left the hotel for good. He'd delayed paying his rent the previous day and had cleared out by the time the management went looking for it. He took all of his belongings with him and, unlike before, left no clues as to where he had gone.

By Tuesday, Gianni Versace and his entourage had settled into the mansion on Ocean Drive. Versace was up early that morning. He strolled a few hundred yards to the News Café, his favourite breakfast haunt, and bought some magazines. He was alone, the way he preferred to be when in South Beach – no security, no friends, no hangers-on.

All over South Beach workers were walking or driving to work while those lucky enough to be able to spend the day on the beach were already arriving there. Nobody knows where Andrew Cunanan had slept the night before, or indeed the night before that, but by 8.40am he was loitering on Ocean Drive, opposite the Versace mansion. He'd been watching the mansion from early morning and almost certainly saw Versace leave for his morning stroll. Gianni may have noticed the handsome, scruffily-dressed, young man, hanging around close to his house. If he did it probably meant nothing to him. Miami was as full of scruffily-dressed vagrants as it was of handsome youths. Gianni ambled slowly back to the villa and paused for a short time outside to put his key into the wrought-iron gate at the entrance.

Andrew seized his opportunity. Walking quickly across the street, he moved, almost running, up the steps to where Versace stood with his back to him. Pulling his gun from his pocket, he fired a bullet at point blank range into the base of the designer's skull, ripping into the back of his neck. As Versace turned, Andrew fired a second .40 calibre bullet into his face. The two rounds literally blew Gianni Versace away. He crumpled in a bloody mess on the steps of his home.

Andrew walked swiftly from the scene, turning left onto 12th street and then right into an alleyway. He was pursued momentarily by a passer-by who gave up the chase when Andrew pointed the gun at him – then he disappeared.

Within minutes the police were on the scene. Their first reaction was confusion – why would anyone want to commit a homicide on the steps of Gianni Versace's mansion? It soon became clear that the victim was actually Versace himself.

The word spread fast and within the hour the story was leading most news bulletins in the United States and news channels across the world. In the gay community the word spread like wildfire – the story that a major gay icon had been assassinated in a gay enclave such as South Beach was big news. One South Beach resident described the impact on the gay community as being similar to the impact in New York when Andy Warhol died. There were open displays of emotion for the dead Versace and devotees began to arrive with floral tributes. They were prevented from putting them on the actual steps by forensic teams who had moved rapidly to seal off the area.

Witnesses explained that they had seen Andrew running down the alley in the direction of the parking garage. It was one of the first places combed by police search teams. Within half an hour of the shooting William Reese's pick-up had been singled out for special attention because a pile of clothes was lying on the ground beside the passenger door. A check of the vehicle's plates threw up the information that the pick-up wasn't just stolen but that it was linked to a major crime. Very quickly the police established the link to Andrew Cunanan.

By the time the evening news bulletins came on-air the Versace story was the number one news item globally. Andrew Cunanan was, for the moment at least, the most famous killer on the planet. The American and international media went wild in an orgy of presumption, suspicion and conspiracy theories. As a result the gay community of South Beach was wound-up into a frenzy and many began to leave the area, taking refuge with friends or relatives in neighbouring cities. Andrew had struck randomly before, he had also struck deliberately at three homosexuals – no one felt safe.

Doctors, meanwhile, had carried out the required state autopsy on the remains of Gianni Versace. His brother Santo, and sister, Donatella, supervised the embalming and subsequent cremation of the remains before they themselves left the Miami area carrying with them the ashes of the city's most famous gay resident.

For the Versaces, and Donatella in particular, the death of her beloved Gianni was a devastating blow. She knew that he had been the object of some attention from a variety of fans and was a particularly attractive icon to the gay community. She had been afraid for some time that he would eventually fall foul of an obsessive person: perhaps someone who might want to extort money from him; or even that he might be the subject of a kidnapping. She had never, however, dreamt that such mindless violence would be visited upon her family. Nor did she ever think that one person could stalk her brother so single-mindedly with only one end in sight.

As the world discussed the murder and the networks tried to find out more about the elusive Andrew Cunanan, he vanished. Not for the first time since Jeff Trail's murder, almost three months earlier, police had no idea where he was hiding or what he might look like at this stage. 'The Andrew Cunanan master of disguise stories' resurfaced. Andrew was hot news and while many gays fled South Beach or fitted new locks on their doors, most believed that he had left the area. They believed that he wouldn't hang around in the face of such intense police activity.

In fact Andrew couldn't have remained closer to the investigation. On the afternoon of Thursday, July 23, eight days after the murder, a caretaker making his rounds of the exclusive Indian Creek Canal checked on a private houseboat moored there. Noticing the door to the houseboat was open, the caretaker boarded and was confronted by a young man who promptly ran into a bedroom and slammed the door. The caretaker rang the police and told them that he suspected that the man on the boat was the fugitive they were looking for. News footage of the subsequent siege of the boat shows an FBI SWAT team of at least twenty officers, backed up by regular police and detectives armed to the teeth. Snipers took up positions on the roofs of nearby apartment blocks and police boats and helicopters hovered nearby – whoever was on the boat was unlikely to escape and if it was Andrew Cunanan they weren't going to let him slip through their fingers.

Three hours later when repeated orders to leave the houseboat met with refusal, the FBI stormed the boat using smoke grenades. Upstairs they found a semi-naked body, propped up on a couple of pillows, dead from a bullet wound through the mouth. Andrew Cunanan's killing spree was over.

Andrew Cunanan differs from most stalkers in one fundamental way – his final, and most high profile, victim was not the sole object of his love, hatred, or all-consuming obsession. The violent death of Gianni Versace was the last in a series of seemingly random murders performed by a disturbed and highly complex individual who, like almost all stalkers, wanted to be anyone but himself. If one were to classify Andrew Cunanan according to police classification, he would undoubtedly be categorised first and foremost as a stalker, but could also probably sit alongside the most recognised serial killers of the 20th century. What sets him apart is the ruthless way in which he single-mindedly chose, followed and then eliminated his ultimate prey. One apparent motive seemed to be envy, that Versace was killed as some type of sick payback for having a more successful, wealthy and famous homosexual lifestyle than Andrew. It was a situation made even more acute by the fact that Andrew had once tasted this rarefied life. According to Eric Hickey, Professor Of Criminology at UCLA:

> 'If you take a look at the dynamics of the killing, he was basically killing the person he could never be… By doing this he not only got to validate his own superiority, he got to make a statement.'

Other educated speculation suggested that Cunanan's motive for stalking and then killing Gianni Versace was revenge. The reasons for that revenge remain unclear. There were certainly rumours following the killing that Versace may have been sexually involved with Cunanan and certainly there is evidence of Vesace recognising Andrew at San Francisco's Colossus Club in 1990. It was also said that he had once rejected Cunanan for a fashion shoot. If the stories of a brief sexual encounter between the two, followed by a rejection by the designer, are true, then they go a long way to explain Cunanan's single-minded obsession with seeking out, and then destroying Versace. If the story, however scurrilous it may be, that Versace was HIV positive at the time of his death, is true, then it might make the concept of Andrew as a revenge stalker very credible.

However, these suppositions are conjecture and were probably a result of the homosexual and media rumour machine working overtime in the wake of a most outrageous and high-profile killing. What is more likely is that a fragile, delusional and troubled loner was finally pushed over the edge of the sanity cliff by his involvement in a homosexual love-triangle. His subsequent cross-country killing spree, in which two other innocent men were murdered, was probably motivated by a combination of robbery and a newly developed interest in killing. His dealings with Versace, however, stand apart from the other killings, as horrific as they may be. Cunanan spent a significant amount of time in Miami, lying low, planning his next move and getting to know how Versace lived his life and went about his daily business. When Andrew set his sights on Gianni Versace, years of resentment came to the surface. A deeply complex and delusionally disordered personality had developed a need to kill – Versace never stood a chance.

CHAPTER SEVEN

I Will Always Love You

One of the most notorious and celebrated stalking cases of recent times featured three main players – a famous Hollywood actress, the President of the United States, and a delusional and obsessive young man who was to become intrinsically linked to both of them.

John Warnock Hinckley, Jr is a very complex man. Born in Ardmore, Oklahoma, on May 29, 1955, John was the youngest of three children. John W. Hinckley, Sr., known as Jack, became the Chairman and President of the enormously successful Vanderbilt Energy Corporation. John's mother Jo Ann, was a housewife who devoted all her time to her children. Hinckley's brother, Scott, graduated from Vanderbilt University and eventually became Vice-President of his father's oil and gas business. Hinckley's sister, Diane, was a popular, straight 'A' student and a graduate of SMU in Dallas. The family was wealthy, socially established and, from the outset, heading very much in the right direction.

When John was four years old, the Hinckley family moved to Dallas, Texas. During his elementary school years John was a normal, happy child. He mixed well, played sport, and was co-operative with teachers and staff. He's remembered particularly as one of the boys who didn't get into fights.

In the early 1960s, when Hinckley was in the sixth grade, his family moved to the exclusive suburb of Highland Park. Their new home boasted luxuries such as a swimming pool and a private *Coke* machine. At his Junior High School, John was elected President of his seventh and ninth grade classes. He was great at sports; he was the quarterback of the school football team and also played basketball. He also helped to manage the school football team and became interested in music and started playing the guitar. His parents noticed that, although he had become very accomplished, he was too shy to play his music in front of anyone,

It was during his later High School years that Hinckley started to change socially. He became withdrawn, almost reclusive, and rarely brought friends home or went out to meet anyone. He abandoned all of his athletic activities, never went out with girls and began to spend most of his time alone in his room, playing his guitar and listening to music, especially *The Beatles*.

John's reclusive lifestyle and increasingly strange behaviour was a worry for Jack and Jo Ann. They attributed his lack of social interaction to shyness. Their friends told them how lucky they were because their son was not drinking or taking drugs. Their friends were struggling with kids who were running around with a rowdy crowd or experimenting with drugs or sex. From the outside John Hinckley appeared responsible, if a bit quiet. His parents and their friends put his unusual behaviour down to adolescent angst. They imagined he would grow out of it.

Psychologists later wondered whether Hinckley withdrew from other people because his thoughts were becoming increasingly strange, perhaps as the result of imbalances in his brain chemistry; Or did his thoughts become disordered because of a lack of perspective as a result of his solitary lifestyle? The theory was later proposed that it could have been a combination of both. As John later said himself of his High School times: 'The atmosphere affected me... I was becoming more rebellious and uncommunicative'. As he finished High School he saw himself as a 'rebel without a cause'.

In 1973, after graduating from High School, John's family moved again. They settled in Evergreen in Colorado. It is a small town on the south-west of the state capital, Denver. This rapidly growing city was to be the new headquarters for his father's business. It was not a town that would hold John's attention for too long.

In the autumn of 1973 he enrolled at Texas Technical University, at Lubbock, to study Business Administration. Lubbock is a medium-sized town located in the northwestern part of Texas, close to the New Mexico border. After finishing his first year, John had the choice of returning to Evergreen or staying in Texas. He opted to move in with his sister, Diane and her husband and son, who had settled in Dallas.

In 1975, John returned to Texas Tech during the spring term. His appearance had deteriorated significantly, transforming him from a thin, friendly young boy to an overweight, uncooperative, moody man. According to later testimony the caretaker of his building once arrived at his apartment for a maintenance job only to discover empty food cartons and rubbish strewn all around the place. According to the caretaker, 'he just sat there the whole time, eating and staring at the TV'.

A year later, in April 1976, still reclusive and without indicating what he was going to do to anyone, John suddenly dropped out of college and flew to California to pursue his dream of becoming a songwriter.

He moved into an apartment in Hollywood and thought about bombarding record companies and agents with demos. He didn't manage to actually do anything. He was later to testify that it was while in Hollywood that he first saw the movie *Taxi Driver*. It made such an impression on him that he went to see it fifteen times that summer. Martin Scorcese's Academy Award winning movie tells the story of an American psychopath who stalks a political candidate. Robert De Niro plays 'Travis Bickle', a Vietnam veteran and insomniac who drives a cab in sleazy, nighttime New York City. He becomes infatuated with pretty and wholesome 'Betsy', played by Cybil Shepherd. She eventually agrees to go out with him. When he takes her to an X-rated movie she leaves him, disgusted, and refuses to see him again. He becomes consumed by loneliness.

The movie was partly inspired by Arthur Bremer who had attempted to assassinate presidential candidate George Wallace. The incident left the radical and racist Wallace disabled for life. According to Bremer's diaries, he too had offended and lost a girlfriend when he showed her pornography. In *Taxi Driver*, Bickle turns to young 'Iris' for friendship. Played by Jodie Foster, Iris is a twelve-year-old prostitute, worldly, yet vulnerable. Bickle dreams of rescuing her from her pimp. He begins arming himself and stalking a popular political candidate. After his plan to shoot him is foiled, Bickle then kills Iris's pimp, the sleazy hotel manager, and one of the customers. These acts of a clearly crazed man are interpreted by the public as heroic and Bickle becomes famous. Iris is freed from the imprisonment of prostitution. The movie was to have a life-changing effect on John Hinckley.

At this time Hinckley's letters to his parents described in detail a non-existent girlfriend, whom he called Lynn Collins. He said she was a young actress from an affluent family. She appeared to have been modelled somewhat on 'Betsy' from *Taxi Driver*. John also told Jack and Jo Ann that he had recently recorded a professional demo of his songs at a recording studio in Los Angeles. He said he was progressing well, making good contacts in the record business and speaking daily with agents who were very interested in his work. They were convinced that he had a future in the business. He told his parents that they would be reading about his musical talents very soon. In reality, Hinckley had no demo and had made no contacts whatsoever in the music business. Shortly after these letters John abruptly left Los Angeles. He was frustrated with what he called the 'phony, impersonal Hollywood scene'.

In September 1976, John returned to his confused parents in Evergreen. He spent his time sitting around in solitude. Eventually he took a job working at the Taylor Supper Club for a few months. Electing not to live with his parents, he moved into a motel across the street from the restaurant.

A sudden and complete change of scene had started to become a feature of Hinckley's behavioural pattern. The obsessive side of his personality was beginning to emerge. The 'stop-start' nature of his obsessive interest in music, then study, and then movies clearly illustrated this development.

In the spring of 1977, he went back to California, determined to try another fresh start. He wanted a final chance at a career in the music business. Once again he disliked the life there and got fed up quickly. Within a year he had decided to resume his studies at Texas Tech.

John made the trip back to Lubbock in the summer of 1978. Living off-campus in an apartment, his attendance at classes became very erratic and he spent long stretches alone. He attended the Tech Clinic on a regular basis with complaints about his eyes, throat and ears, and a constant feeling of light-headedness. Doctors prescribed anti-depressants and tranquilisers, noting that John had a 'flat affect throughout examination and depressive reaction'. There is no doubt that Hinckley was lonely throughout his entire time in Lubbock. He was slow to make any friends and spent most of his time on his own, thinking. In a letter to his sister Diane in Dallas he wrote:

> 'My nervous system is about shot, I take heavy medication for it which doesn't seem to do much good except make me very drowsy. By the end of the summer, I should be a bona fide basket case.'

He later testified that it was at this time that he began to fantasize about *Taxi Driver* and about Jodie Foster in particular.

The concept of 'Bickle' 'setting Iris free...' appealed to John Hinckley. There may even have been a personal desire, not only to set the movie 'Iris' free, but also for Hinckley to release Jodie Foster from what he perceived to be her imprisonment in the movies, in Hollywood or wherever else his mind suggested. He began collecting guns just as Travis Bickle did in 'Taxi Driver'. He purchased his first gun, a .38 calibre pistol, in August 1979 and began his own private target practice.

For Christmas 1979, he decided not to return to Evergreen for the holidays, telling his parents that he was meeting the fictional Lynn in New York. In fact he stayed in Lubbock, watching television and occasionally playing Russian Roulette with a loaded pistol. A photograph was later discovered showing him holding the gun to his head. For the next year, he continued to add to his gun collection, and bought a case of exploding-head devastator bullets from a pawnshop in Lubbock. John Hinckley was getting prepared for whatever was coming next. The main object of his attention, meanwhile, was fast becoming one of Hollywood's hottest female stars.

Alicia Christian Foster was born on November 19, 1962, in Los Angeles, California. She was nicknamed 'Jodie', after her mother's friend, 'Josephine D'. Her father, Lucius, left the family before she was born, leaving her mother Evelyn, nicknamed 'Brandy', to raise Foster and three older kids. Brandy was a Hollywood publicist and from an early age Jodie was closely associated with the movie industry. Her first screen appearance was at the age of three. She appeared in a *Coppertone sun lotion* television commercial. From then on, she was rarely short of work. Offers in television and movies kept rolling in and she made a number of child feature films with Disney Studios.

By 1972, ten-year-old Jodie Foster was a major child star. Agents and producers across the United States knew her name. Her earnings were so strong that her mother gave up her job to manage Jodie's career full-time. Brandy Foster had spent long enough in the entertainment industry to have a 'grounded' view of it. She saw a more than average intelligence in her young daughter and was determined that education would not be forgotten. Brandy knew that acting in Hollywood might easily be a very short-term career. Between acting jobs Foster was a regular student and attended the Los Angeles' Lycée Francais, where she became fluent in French. Her time at the Lycée also helped to broaden her already successful career by allowing Jodie to act in French films.

Jodie Foster was only fourteen when Martin Scorsese cast her as 'Iris' in *Taxi Driver*. The controversial role won Jodie critical acclaim and led to her first Oscar nomination for Best Supporting Actress. She had reached the pinnacle of the movie industry and was a major box office property.

Determined to lead a normal life in tandem with her acting career, Jodie completed High School at the Lycée Francais, graduating in 1980 at the top of her class. This was no mean feat for someone who was spending six months of her year on a film set. Throughout her school years she had played, among other roles, Miss Tallulah, a bawdy speakeasy diva, in the children's spoof movie *Bugsy Malone* and a young murderer in the 1977 film *The Little Girl who lived down the Lane.*

Following her High School graduation, Foster moved to New Haven, Connecticut, where she enrolled to study English literature at Yale University. For a movie star to pursue a college career *after* making it in Hollywood was unusual to say the least and Jodie and her family knew it would be difficult for her to simply blend into the student body. She was determined to try but the media coverage of a movie star moving to study at Yale was huge.

John Hinckley was still obsessed with Jodie Foster and even more specifically with her role as 'Iris', so many years earlier. When he read in May 1980 that Foster was enrolling at Yale, he told his parents he wanted to join a writing course at the university. They were pleased that he had a new 'goal' and gave him the $3,600 enrolment fee without hesitation. He'd been behaving so strangely of late that they wanted to do whatever they could to help him find a career and, hopefully, make some friends.

John immediately left for Connecticut, certain that he would finally get to meet Foster. He believed that she needed rescuing from her plight and that he, John Hinckley, was the person to do it. In his mind he saw her as Iris, the vulnerable twelve-year-old prostitute, not as a nineteen-year-old movie star turned student, now attending one of the most prestigious Ivy League colleges in the United States.

When John arrived in New Haven, he asked around the campus and was able to get Foster's address without much difficulty. The publicity about her arrival was such that, unknown to her, every student, academic and pizza delivery boy in New Haven had a rough idea where she lived. John had prepared himself for a long search and was somewhat surprised when tracking her down was so easy. It also concerned him a little. If he had found her, then others might just as easily track her down. Getting through to Jodie was his mission and he didn't want anyone else interfering with it.

Feeling too shy to contact her face-to-face, John decided to write to her. He left a series of letters and poems in her mailbox. John continued to fantasize about Jodie Foster. While staying locally in a hotel he spent some time tracking down her phone number. He had obviously decided that stalking her through the mail just wasn't enough to feed his obsession. Eventually he managed to get her phone number and called her twice. Jodie was clearly shocked that he'd been able to access her number and politely, but firmly told him to leave her alone. Hinckley recorded one of the conversations. On the tape, Jodie Foster said:

> 'I can't carry on these conversations with people I don't know. It's dangerous, and it's just not done, and it's not fair, and it's rude.'

He replied: 'I'm not dangerous, I promise you that.'
Getting nowhere in his search for a 'relationship' with

Foster, at some point Hinckley clearly decided that he would only win her respect by gaining fame or notoriety. She would surely sit up and take notice if he killed somebody important, just like his hero 'Bickle' had attempted in *Taxi Driver*. Sometime that autumn, in some part of John's delusional mind, he decided to assassinate the President of the United States so that Jodie Foster would fall in love with him.

Late 1980 was a difficult enough time for the President. Jimmy Carter, the peanut farmer from Plains, Georgia, had swept to power on a tide of anti-Nixon sentiment following the Watergate scandal and the President's resignation in 1974. The short-term, ineffective, presidency of Nixon's Vice-President, the hapless Gerald Ford, had done little to restore public confidence in a Republican administration. It had virtually assured Carter's victory. He had promised a clean start and an accountable presidency. Now, straining under the burden of fifty-two American citizens being held by Iranian Islamic fundamentalists at the US embassy in Tehran, as well as a faltering economy, Jimmy Carter looked increasingly unlikely to be re-elected in the November 4 poll.

Hinckley began to stalk President Carter with the intention of shooting him. Carter was attending election rallies in three cities and Hinckley followed him to each one: on September 27, 1980 he went to Washington DC; on September 28 to Columbus, Ohio; on September 30 to Dayton, again in Ohio. A videotape which was later played at Hinckley's trial, demonstrated that John successfully stalked Carter. It showed him standing less than six feet away from the President. He got this close but in each city Hinckley was unable to bring himself to shoot Carter.

After Dayton, Hinckley flew to Lincoln, Nebraska,

where he claimed he had arranged to meet the leader of the American Nazi Party. The following day he travelled to Nashville, Tennessee, where another Carter campaign rally was planned for October 7. While passing through Nashville airport, en route to New York, security detected three guns and thirty rounds of ammunition in Hinckley's suitcase, as well as $800 in his wallet. He was arrested and his guns were confiscated. As the guns were legally held, Hinckley was fined $62.50, for the offence of carrying them through the airport, and released. Undeterred, he bought two more guns, .22 calibre handguns, at a pawnshop called Rocky's in Dallas.

Upset and frustrated, Hinckley returned to Evergreen. Clearly directionless and depressed, he now had to face his parents. They told him in no uncertain terms how disappointed they were about his lack of achievement. This was the last straw. He was going nowhere, the object of his love had rejected him and his attempts to gain respect in her eyes had been denied by his own failure to take advantage of the opportunity to kill Carter when it had presented itself.

In late October, John attempted suicide by taking an overdose of antidepressants. This shook Hinckley's parents enough to send their increasingly disturbed son to see Dr John Hopper, a psychiatrist in Colorado. Any trust between doctor and patient evaporated when Hinckley discovered that Dr Hopper discussed their sessions with his parents. Thereafter John withheld any information he considered private from their sessions.

Hinckley attended about a dozen sessions with Dr Hopper, giving some clues to indicate his obsessive behavioural patterns. By all accounts, and according to subsequent testimony, the doctor failed to pick up on them. In early November he told Hopper about his feelings

for Jodie Foster. In another session, he told him about
the trip he had made to Yale to see Foster. He said his
mind 'was at breaking point the whole time'. He went on
to explain, 'a relationship I had dreamed about went
absolutely nowhere. My disillusionment was complete.'
It would later transpire that Dr Hopper did not pursue
any of these angles with his patient.

In 1980, Hinckley sent an anonymous note to the FBI
which read:

> 'There is a plot underway to abduct actress
> Jodie Foster from Yale University dorm in
> December or January. No ransom. She's being
> taken for romantic reasons. This is no joke ! I
> don't wish to get further involved. Act as you
> wish.'

On December 8, 1980, an event occurred which deeply
affected John Hinckley. John Lennon, one of his all time
musical heroes, was shot and killed outside his home in
New York by Mark Chapman. Hinckley immediately took
a train to New York. He joined in an all-night vigil for
Lennon outside the singer's apartment building. He noted
later that he went into 'deep mourning' and was completely
traumatised by the shooting. The experience also had a
bizarre counter-reaction. Hinckley later admitted that he
began in some way to identify with Mark Chapman. He
went out and bought a Charter Arms .38 calibre revolver
similar to the one that Chapman had used to assassinate
Lennon.

Mark Chapman fascinated Hinckley. Here was someone
who had sought out his prey and followed through on his
intentions. On reading that Chapman had travelled from
as far away as Hawaii to stalk, and eventually assassinate

Lennon, Hinckley was impressed. He was also disappointed with himself. He'd followed President Carter and had fallen apart just as the opportunity to 'prove' himself to Jodie Foster had presented itself. On hearing that Chapman had taken much of his inspiration and life ideas from J D Salinger's *The Catcher in the Rye*, John acquired a copy. He tried to relate to Chapman by relating to his idol Holden Caulfield. Mark Champan's example had certainly convinced John that the next time he tried to do something he would do it properly.

Over the next few months, and back in Colorado, John continued his sessions with Dr Hopper. He wasn't totally committed to getting treatment. He frequently didn't show up for appointments. Instead he spent hours practising his shooting skills and writing letters and poems to Jodie Foster. Periodically he would take a plane to New York and travel from there to New Haven to deliver his missives personally, to Foster's campus mailbox. He was later to admit that on these occasions he often went to Manhattan to look for prostitutes that he might 'rescue'. Inevitably they were more interested in taking this strange guy on as a client rather than being 'saved' by him. He obliged at least four times, mostly with teenage prostitutes.

By New Year's Eve he was sufficiently depressed to record the following on a cassette tape which is now reproduced on crimelibrary.com:

> 'John Lennon is dead. The world is over. Forget it. It's just gonna be insanity, if I even make it through the first few days... I still regret having to go on with 1981... I don't know why people wanna live.
>
> John Lennon is dead... I still think-I still think about Jodie all the time. That's all I

think about really. That, and John Lennon's death. They were sorta binded together...

I hate New Haven with a mortal passion. I've been up there many times, not stalking her really, but just looking after her.... I was going to take her away for a while there, but I don't know. I am so sick I can't even do that. ... It'll be total suicide city. I mean, I couldn't care less. Jodie is the only thing that matters now. Anything I might do in 1981 would be solely for Jodie Foster's sake.

My obsession is Jodie Foster. I've gotta, I've gotta find her and talk to her some way in person or something.... That's all I want her to know, is that I love her. I don't want to hurt her... I think I'd rather just see her not, not on earth, than being with other guys. I wouldn't want to stay here on earth without her.'

On February 14, 1981, St Valentine's Day, Hinckley was in Manhattan again. He visited the Dakota Building intending to commit suicide on the street outside it. He couldn't do it and returned home to his parents in Colorado.

On February 27 he went to Dr Hopper for his last appointment. Dr Hopper concluded that his problem stemmed from emotional immaturity and he needed to learn to shoulder adult responsibilities. He recommended to Hinckley's parents that they adopt a 'tough love' approach with their son and cut him off financially. Dr Hopper believed that the Hinckleys had to force John to make it on his own. Together they set March 1 as the date by which John would have to find a job. This was

only days away and would have been a tall order for even
the most qualified job candidate. For John, in his current
state of mental confusion, it was an unrealistic deadline.
March 30 was set as the deadline when Hinckley would
have to leave his parent's home. His parents then went
away for a short time. They returned home on March 1
to find a note stuck to their door. It said, 'Your prodigal
son has left again, I must exorcise some demons'.

John had gone to Yale to deliver another batch of
letters and poems to Jodie Foster. They ranged in content
from genuinely romantic to bizarrely pathetic:

> 'Jodie,
> GOODBYE! I love you six trillion times.
> DON'T YOU MAYBE LIKE ME A LITTLE
> BIT? (YOU MUST ADMIT IT I AM
> DIFFERENT).
> It would make all the difference.
> JOHN HINCKLEY
>
> Guns are Fun!
> See that living legend over there?
> With one little squeeze of this trigger
> I can put that person at my feet
> moaning and groaning and pleading with God.
> This gun gives me pornographic power.
> If I wish, the president will fall
> and the world will look at me in disbelief,
> all because I own an inexpensive gun.
> Guns are lovable, Guns are fun
> Are you lucky enough to own one?
>
> I Know a Girl
> I know a girl who is beyond words;

I don't know her well but I know her.
I know she knows that I know her
and she knows that I love her.
I don't know her true feelings towards me
but she knows that I know her name.
Amen

Jodie isn't plastic nor does she cry
at the sight of me writhing in pain
down in the gutter of Anystreet USA
because Jodie will always be Jodie.
Don't cry for me Arizona
the truth is

I brought it on myself
in a calculated way
and by means which
I would postively hurt
everyone around me.

The Painful Evolution
In the beginning
it was a time for pretending.
The martyr in me played games
and I was the young alienated loner.'

Other letters included lines such as 'Wait for me, I will rescue you'. The words resonated with the same thoughts and ideas expressed in the fictional letters 'Bickle' sends to 'Iris' in *Taxi Driver*. The content of Hinckley's latest batch of letters concerned Foster so much that she handed them over to the Dean of her College. She had clearly come to the conclusion that she was been stalked by a potentially dangerous individual whose obsessive passion was out of control.

From New Haven, Hinckley went back to New York City. On March 7 he hired a limousine to drive him from Manhattan to Newark Airport in New Jersey. He was flying back to Denver. He rang home from the airport and asked his parents to meet him off the plane. He made the call at 4.30am and was in an incoherent state. His father went to meet his flight while Jo Ann stayed at home, racked with guilt about the forthcoming confrontation. They had agreed to tell John that he was no longer allowed to live in his own home.

At Denver Airport Jack could see his son was in bad shape. He hadn't shaved and was physically very weak. His eyes were glazed over and it was clear that he hadn't been sleeping or eating properly. Determined to abide by Dr Hopper's recommendations, Hinckley Senior talked to his son. He told John how disappointed they were that he hadn't followed their agreed plan and that he still hadn't found a job. Instead of driving home, he drove John to his own car which was parked at the airport. He told John that he couldn't come home, suggesting instead that he stay at a YMCA. According to Jack Hinckley:

> 'He looked at me as if he couldn't believe his
> ears. I gave him $200 and suggested that the
> YMCA is an inexpensive place to live.'

But John didn't want to live at the YMCA. In the end Jack said, 'Well it's your decision, John, from here on out, do whatever you want to do'. Looking back, Jack now feels that forcing his son out of his home at a time when he just couldn't cope was the greatest mistake of his life. He now thinks that it most likely contributed in a major way to the events that were about to unfold.

Devastated, John checked into a local motel and stayed there for the next two weeks. He spent his time alone, watching television and reading. However, without his father's knowledge, he did visit his mother at home on a number of occasions. On March 27, he begged her to take him to the airport. She reluctantly obliged. They drove the journey in stony silence. Eventually she broke down crying and gave him some money. As Hinckley took his suitcase he said to her, 'I want to thank you, Mom, for everything you've ever done for me, all these years'. She replied, 'You're very welcome.' and drove off.

Hinckley was confused about what he should do next. He had an idea to go to New Haven and kill himself in front of Jodie Foster. Then he thought he might kill her first and then kill himself. He even toyed with the idea of hijacking a plane and had bought a book *The Skyjacker* on the subject. He also carried a *Band-Aid* box in his jacket pocket containing a hijacking note, which said 'This plane has been hijacked! I have a bomb'.

He finally decided to fly to Los Angeles again and stayed there for one day. The next morning he boarded a cross-country Greyhound bus and headed for Washington DC reaching the Greyhound station in Washington on March 29, at 12.15pm. He checked into room 312 of the Park Central Hotel in Washington. He had two suitcases, a John Lennon calendar, a postcard of Ronald and Nancy Reagan and a variety of pills, including Valium, Surmontil and Drixoral. He also had a selection of books including, *The Catcher in the Rye*, *The Fan*, *Romeo and Juliet* and *Taxi Driver*.

Next day he got up and had breakfast in a fast food outlet near the hotel. He bought the *Washington Star* newspaper on the way back to the hotel and read that President Reagan would be making a speech to 3,500 members of the Construction Workers Union in the Washington Hilton that afternoon. John couldn't believe his luck. Today, Reagan would be in town, away from the White House and John Hinckley would probably be able to get close enough to him to get a clear shot.

The President had been in the White House just three months. Ronald Wilson Reagan had been sworn in as the 40th president of the United States on January 20, 1981. At sixty-nine-years old the affable actor-turned-politician was the oldest incumbent of that office. Reagan was already a popular president. Despite his right-wing economic measures, he was getting favourable treatment in the press, largely because the Iranian authorities had purposely chosen not to release the US hostages until after his inauguration. The move had been devastating for the Carter campaign and had given the Reagan campaign a big advantage. Reagan's kindly face, easy smile and affable manner had already endeared him to the public and press regardless of their politics. Even Reagan's critics tended to poke fun at him in a gentle manner, focusing on such things as his notoriously poor memory and his habit of retiring to watch the television in the White House residence at six each evening.

Hinckley had a shower and loaded his .22 calibre gun with the exploding devastator bullets he'd bought in Lubbock. At around 12.45pm he began writing what he believed would be his final letter to Jodie Foster:

'Dear Jodie,

There is definitely a possibility that I will be killed in my attempt to get Reagan. It is for this very reason that I am writing you this letter now.

As you well know by now I love you very much. Over the past seven months I've left you dozens of poems, letters and love messages in the faint hope that you could develop an interest in me. Although we talked on the phone a couple of times I never had the nerve to simply approach you and introduce myself. Besides my shyness, I honestly did not wish to bother you with my constant presence. I know the many messages left at your door and in your mailbox were a nuisance, but I felt that it was the most painless way for me to express my love for you.

I feel very good about the fact that you at least know my name and how I feel about you. And by hanging around your dormitory, I've come to realise that I'm the topic of more than a little conversation, however full of ridicule it may be. At least you know that I'll always love you. Jodie, I would abandon the idea of getting Reagan in a second if I could only win your heart and live out the rest of my life with you, whether it be in total obscurity or whatever.

I will admit to you that the reason I'm going ahead with this attempt now is because I cannot wait any longer to impress you. I've got to do something now to make you understand, in no uncertain terms, that I'm doing all of this for your sake! By sacrificing my freedom and possibly my life, I hope to change your mind about me. This letter is being written only an hour before I leave for the Hilton Hotel. Jodie, I'm asking you to

please look into your heart and at least give
me the chance, with this historical deed, to
gain your love and respect.

I love you forever,
John Hinckley'

It was raining lightly that afternoon so at 1.30pm
Hinckley took a cab to the Washington Hilton Hotel at
1919 Connecticut Avenue. As Hinckley was arriving the
presidential motorcade, driven by Agent Drew Unrue,
pulled up to the hotel. Reagan waved to the crowd as he
entered the hotel. There was a small police barrier keeping
the small crowd of onlookers back from the hotel doorway
but only by a few feet. Hinckley was surprised he could
get so close to the President. It was business as usual at
the Hilton despite the Presidential appearance and
Hinckley was able to walk in another door unchallenged
and sit in the lobby for ten or fifteen minutes. Then he
returned to his position outside.

At 2.25pm, President Reagan left the Grand Ballroom
and headed towards his waiting limousine. A close Secret
Service detail of some ten agents was around him, led by
Jerry Parr, the special-agent-in-charge and the man
entrusted with the closest protection of the President.
White House Press Secretary, James Brady accompanied
the presidential detail, as did the White House Deputy
Chief of Staff, Mike Deaver. Both were walking a couple
of paces behind Reagan and to his left. As Reagan walked
towards the door of the hotel somebody in the crowd
shouted, 'President Reagan, President Reagan!' As he
turned towards the voice, and also in Hinckley's direction,
waving at the small crowd, Hinckley saw his chance. The
President was no more than ten or fifteen feet away. He

took the gun from his right-hand pocket and crouched into a marksman position, holding his gun in both hands. He quickly fired off six bullets in rapid succession.

The first bullet entered press secretary James Brady's brain over his left eye. The second hit police officer Thomas Delahanty in the neck. The third hit some stone in the building. Turning in the direction of the fire, Secret Service Agent Timothy McCarthy did what he was trained to do. He positioned himself as much as possible in front of the President and took the fourth bullet in the abdomen. The fifth bullet hit the bullet-proof glass of the President's limousine. The sixth and final bullet hit the car but ricocheted off it and hit Reagan under his arm, entering his lung, only inches from his heart.

Jerry Parr's reactions were like lightning. He shoved the President head first into the limousine, landing on top of him as he also dived into the car. Agent Ray Shaddick, the second closest man to the President, slammed the door shut. Drew Unrue, sensing the urgency of the situation, slammed his foot down on the accelerator. The heavy bullet-proofed car took off like a rocket. Reagan cursed at Parr, telling him that he had hurt his ribs on impact. Both were unaware that Reagan had actually been shot. Parr had told Unrue to head straight for the White House, believing it to be the safest place for the President. As they passed through the tunnel under Dupont Circle, the President became distressed and began to cough up blood. Parr immediately instructed Unrue to head for George Washington University Hospital. Parr's actions almost certainly saved President Reagan's life.

When they arrived at the hospital the President was taken to the operating theatre where surgeons worked for two hours. By the evening he was pronounced 'comfortable' and 'out of danger'. By the morning he was back to his old self, joking about his near-death experience, saying to the surgeons, 'I hope you guys are Republicans?' and telling his distraught wife Nancy, 'Sorry Honey, I forgot to duck'.

Back at the Hilton, all hell was breaking loose. People were running around screaming while the wounded were lying around the hotel in pools of blood. The Secret Service Agents, pistols or machine guns drawn, had wrestled Hinckley to the ground while he was still clicking the trigger of his empty gun. He was bundled away, arrested, and quickly identified. Agents found five pictures of Jodie Foster in his wallet and a card with the Second Amendment printed on it, 'the right to bear arms'. He was charged with thirteen crimes including knowing and intentionally attempting to kill the President and assaulting a federal officer. His .22 calibre pistol was taken from him. He was taken to the Metropolitan Police Department and held without bail. Hinckley later asked one of his arresting officers if news of the shooting would go out before that night's Academy Awards broadcast.

Later that evening Officer Delahanty and Agent McCarthy were given the all clear on their injuries and were pronounced 'comfortable'. Doctors feared, however, that James Brady would not survive. It would be many months later, following intense treatment, before doctors were able to declare that Brady was out of danger. But he was severely paralysed and would be confined to a wheelchair for the rest of his life.

At the White House the situation was nothing short of farcical. The Vice-President, George Bush, who was on a visit to Texas that afternoon, had immediately been told about the shooting and was on his way back to Washington aboard Air Force Two. As the President had been rushed to surgery and no formal hand over of power had occurred (which is a requirement in a situation where the President is temporarily incapacitated) Reagan was still technically in charge of the government and the country. In the White House, however, the situation was unclear. Larry Speakes, the Deputy Press Secretary, returned from GWU Hospital in a somewhat agitated state. Without consulting the senior White House staff, who were gathered in the situation room, he went straight to the Press briefing room and began to speak to the media representatives who were grouped there, clamouring for news. He said, 'the President's condition was unclear' and continued to try to field questions on who was running the White House, the Government, and in particular, the nation's defence and nuclear strike capacities. Watching on the internal television system, a number of senior Presidential aides became concerned that Speakes was struggling, particularly in relation to state of alert and readiness of operational forces. In the event of an assassination attempt on the President, the possibility of it being a preamble to a strike by enemy forces is always considered.

At this point, Alexander Haig, the Secretary of State, said 'I had better go up and say something'. Rushing into the hastily arranged press briefing he declared at 4.15pm, 'as of now, I am in control here, in the White House... '. He was not in control. Presidential succession as defined by the Presidential Succession Act of 1947 would have ranked Haig behind not only Bush, as the elected Vice-President, but also behind the Speaker of the House of Representatives and the President Pro-Tem of the Senate. Charitable observers say that Haig was acting on his knowledge of the original Succession Act of 1886. However, given that the statute was updated by the 1947 Act and the twenty-fifth amendment to the Constitution, it is more likely that he just got carried away by a combination of the overall confusion and his own self-importance. According to Martin Anderson, the White House Chief of Domestic Policy Planning, Haig's remarks:

> '... set off an explosion of concern. ... For millions of Americans watching for news of whether President Reagan was alive or dead, Haig's words sounded ominously like a veiled grasp for power'.

Bush's arrival that evening restored some calm but the incident would haunt Haig for the rest of his political career.

John Hinckley's crazed assassination attempt, earlier that afternoon, was having wide ranging consequences. Not only had he succeeded in almost killing one of the most powerful men in the world, he had indirectly caused a major rift in Ronald Reagan's administration. Hinckley had assured that he was the main news story on television, radio and in the press worldwide.

Jo Ann Hinckley was at home watching television when a news flash interrupted the programme. When the newscaster described the incident and went on to describe the assailant as a light-haired man in his twenties, Jo Ann's heart went out to his family. Then the telephone rang. It was a reporter from the *Washington Post* who said:

> 'Mrs Hinckley, do you have your television set on? Do you know your son John Hinckley is the man they have identified as the person who shot the President?'

Jack Hinckley heard the news on the radio after the

gunman had been identified as John Hinckley. His reaction was total disbelief. As he was to later comment:

> 'Getting John to assert himself was always the problem... John just got more listless and inactive all the time. Was this a person who could buy a gun, travel clear across the country, and shoot the President of the United States?'

Jodie Foster was running across the Yale campus with a friend when she heard President Reagan had been shot. At the time, she had no idea that the would-be assassin was the strange man who had been calling her and pestering her with love letters. When Hinckley's motivation became public knowledge and she learned that her photographs and college address were found in his motel room, the news hit her like a ton of bricks. She was very badly shaken. The press arrived down to Yale in droves. Foster later commented that the press had '... swarmed through the campus like a cavalry invasion. I couldn't protect myself from being trampled.' She gave a brief press conference and spoke of her reaction to the shooting. She described how her body:

> '...jerked in painful convulsions. I hurt. I was no longer thinking of the President, of the assailant, of the crime, of the press. I was crying for myself, me, the unwilling victim. The one who would pay in the end. The one who paid all along – and, yes, keeps paying.'

The trial of John Hinckley started a year later, on May 4, 1982. Hinckley insisted that his attorneys get Foster to testify at his trial. If they didn't, he said he would refuse to co-operate with them. Eventually she agreed to testify in a closed session with only the judge, lawyers and Hinckley present, to protect her privacy. This session was taped and shown to the court and the jury.

Foster answered her questions calmly. She told the court that shortly after she started at Yale she had received letters and poems from Hinckley. She said that neither she nor her friends had ever seen the sender. She described the first letters received from John as lovelorn fan mail, of a sort she often received. She got a small parcel of them in September 1980 and a second batch later that year.

Foster told the court she had thrown them away. But when another batch of notes was delivered in March 1981 she noticed that the tone had changed. 'These were a different type of letter,' she explained, 'so I gave it to the Dean of my college.' Her concern was warranted. One letter from that batch said: ' It's all for you, Foster.' Another said, 'Jodie Foster, love, just wait. I will rescue you very soon. Please co-operate. J.W.H.'. She agreed with the court that in the movie *Taxi Driver* the character Travis Bickle also sends her character 'Iris' a similar rescue letter. Foster said she didn't respond to Hinckley's letters. She never invited them and confirmed that she didn't have any relationship with Hinckley.

Hinckley went berserk when Jodie Foster said this. Reacting to what he later described as a 'snub', he shouted at Foster 'I'll get you', and tried to run over to her. Security marshals in the court jumped to restrain him. When the tape of their telephone conversation was played in the courtroom, Hinckley went mad again. He jumped up screaming and waving his arms trying to shout down the words as they played. He tried to run out of the court and the court marshals again had to restrain him.

Hinckley's defence team also showed the movie *Taxi Driver* in the courtroom. Hinckley's reaction to the movie demonstrated the depth of the impression it had made on him; twisting in his chair to get a better look at Robert DeNiro's face as it appeared on the screen, he became so engrossed that he watched it with his mouth open, eyes locked on the screen. He took his eyes away from the screen only twice. The first time was when Betsy turns Travis down for a date – at this point Hinckley took off his glasses and turned his head aside. The second time was when Iris, played by Jodie Foster, embraced her pimp – at this point he turned his head away from the screen completely.

On June 21, 1982, after more that seven weeks of testimony and three days of deliberation by the jury each of the seven women and five men gave the same verdict on all thirteen counts, including attempted murder on six counts and attempted assassination of a president. John Hinckley Jr was pronounced not guilty by reason of insanity. The whole courtroom was shocked by the verdict. Observers had believed that a guilty verdict was a foregone conclusion and nobody, including John's defence attorneys, had expected a not guilty verdict. They had pinned their few hopes on one early advantage.

Judge Parker had ruled that the burden of proof regarding Hinckley's mental status would rest with the prosecution. So, it had been down to the District Attorney to prove beyond a reasonable doubt that John Hinckley was legally sane when he shot the President. Some jurors had felt the suicidal tendencies in his letters to Jodie Foster had definitely indicated insanity. Others felt his attempts to get money from his parents had clearly demonstrated that he was sane. They differed, however, on how to interpret his continuous travelling across the

United States. One juror argued:

> 'Nobody, no matter how much money he has
> would spend it like that. He pays a jet fare
> and stays a day. I can't see that.'

But another said:

> 'Anytime you can buy airplane tickets and go
> anywhere you want and get the money to do
> it, you're sane.'

Hinckley was remanded immediately and committed
to St Elizabeth's Hospital in Washington, a facility operated
by the United States Department of Mental Health. He
underwent a psychiatric evaluation and was classified a
danger to himself and to Jodie Foster. Despite privileges
allowing him day trips to shopping malls, bookshops and
restaurants, Hinckley remains a patient at St Elizabeth's
to this day.

In spite of his hospitalisation, Hinckley was determined
not to fade from the public spotlight. Shortly after he
was committed to St Elizabeth's, he gave an interview to
Penthouse magazine in which he described a typical day
there:

> 'I see a therapist, answer mail, play my guitar,
> listen to music, play pool, watch television,
> eat lousy food, and take delicious medication.'

Following the assassination attempt and subsequent
trial of John Hinckley, Dr John Hopper was sued by the
victims of Hinckley's shooting spree, with the notable
exception of President Reagan. In court, James Brady,

Thomas Delahanty, and Timothy McCarthy alleged that Dr Hopper had inadequately treated John Hinckley. Their action sought $14 million in damages. They also claimed that Hopper, as a psychiatric professional, should have recognised Hinckley was a danger and a threat to society and ensured that he was committed to a mental hospital. They argued that Hopper failed to warn police of the possibility that Hinckley would attempt a political assassination despite Hinckley's admission that his 'mind was at breaking point'. The suit was later dismissed. The United States District Court ruled that because Hinckley never threatened anybody, Dr Hopper could not have known that Hinckley was dangerous or warned Brady and the others of a potential danger.

In 1985, Hinckley himself went to court to seek an order lifting hospital bans on his access to phones and 'grounds privileges' – the opportunity to walk on hospital grounds accompanied by a staff member. Hinckley testified as follows:

> 'Your Honor, I can see now that I did need that interview restriction in the summer of '82 because my judgment was poor and my delusions about Jodie Foster were so strong that I was capable of saying some very dangerous things. But now my doctors and I believe that my judgment is much better and my obsession with Jodie Foster has been over for 19 months....
>
> I think I am ready, too, for limited ground privileges.... I deserve [such] privileges now because my doctors say I am clinically ready for them. It should not take more than a week or two to work out the security precautions. I

would be willing to wear a bulletproof vest and walk with an armed guard if that is what the hospital and court wants.

All I want is the chance to have my therapy in the sunshine for a change away from the walls and fences and bars and every other depressing thing. The atmosphere at John Howard Pavilion can be suffocating at times and it would be the best therapy in the world for me to breathe fresh air away from that building an hour a day or an hour a week if the court feels that is more appropriate.

Your Honor, it has been two and one-half years since the assassination attempt and a lot has happened during that time. I spent 13 months in a very depressed state of mind waiting for trial.

On June 21, 1982 I was found not guilty by reason of insanity and the next day I was taken to St Elizabeth's Hospital to begin my recovery. My first six months at the hospital were bleak because I was still obsessed, depressed and desperate.

At the height of my despair on February 13, 1983, I attempted suicide and, thank God, I failed. Nothing has been the same since that suicide attempt.

I overcame the obsession with Jodie Foster through intense therapy, medication and a lot of love from the people around me. For the first time in years I was glad to be alive and each day became an exciting challenge and adventure.

I now cherish my life and believe that

everyone's life is sacred and precious. I will never again harm another human being. On the issue of giving interviews to the media... I would like to be able to give an occasional interview to media representatives whom I can trust, but the hospital says no to any patient giving interviews. It is quite obvious that the interview restriction at St Elizabeth's was written up with John Hinckley in mind. I am, of course, the most well-known patient at the hospital and just about the only patient that the media cares about and wants to interview. ...

Your Honor, I am ready for some responsibility. I am asking you to lift the interview and telephone restrictions and let me walk the grounds of the hospital accompanied by staff. Please give me the opportunity to prove to you and the hospital and the entire world that I am getting well.

Thank you.'

After the hearing, Judge Parker denied Hinckley's request for the termination of the hospital's restrictive policies.

In 1987, Hinckley applied for leave to visit his family at Easter, and Judge Parker ordered a search of his room; it revealed twenty banned photographs and writings which revealed he was still obsessed with Jodie Foster. It also uncovered letters to his pen-pals who included the serial killer Ted Bundy.

As a direct result of Hinckley's trial and many people's perception that justice was not done, the case has continued to gain even more notoriety and media attention. It directly led to legislation changes limiting the use of the insanity plea in several American states. Within a month of the Hinckley verdict, the House of Representatives and the United States Senate had held hearings on the treatment of insanity as a defence.

A measure was proposed to shift the burden of proof of insanity to the defence. Two thirds of the States had signed up for this measure within three years of Hinckley's trial. Several States rewrote their statutes and laws to tighten up the standards for insanity and restrict its use as a defence. Montana, Idaho and Utah abolished the defence of insanity altogether. Twelve years after the assassination attempt, President Clinton signed the Brady Bill (named in honour of James Brady), which requires a waiting period and background check on all handguns purchased through licensed dealers.

Jodie Foster had no sooner dealt with one stalker when, shortly after Hinckley's arrest, another obsessed fan, Edward Michael Richardson, placed her firmly back in the spotlight. He decided to finish what Hinckley had set out to do. Richardson was on his way to Washington DC when he was arrested by Federal authorities. He was carrying a loaded gun. He later told police that he was obsessed with Jodie Foster. He had initially gone to Yale with the idea of killing her but after following her around the campus for a while, he had decided that she was 'too pretty'. He changed his mind and decided to shoot the President instead.

After this experience Jodie Foster retreated almost completely from the public spotlight. She became, and remains to this day, one of Hollywood's most private celebrities. She refuses to comment on the Hinckley incident, restricting interviews to questions about her career and terminating them if the subject is ever raised.

She returned to student life and graduated from Yale in 1985 with an honours degree. She continued to make movies becoming big news again in 1988 when she starred with Kelly McGillis in the controversial movie *The Accused*. It was one of her finest performances and it earned her a Golden Globe and her first Oscar for Best Actress. She then made Hollywood history, in 1991, by winning a second Best Actress Oscar for her role as FBI rookie agent Clarice Starling in *The Silence of the Lambs*, thus becoming the first person to win two Oscars before reaching their thirtieth birthday.

Today Jodie Foster is acknowledged as one of the most powerful women in Hollywood. She has become one of its highest paid actresses and directors. In 1998 she gave birth to her first son, Charles, and in 2001 just after she finished filming the thriller *The Panic Room*, she gave birth to her second child, Kit.

Over two decades since the assassination attempt in 1981, John Hinckley spends his days on a tree-lined estate. Since 1990 Hinckley has been romantically involved with Leslie deVeau, whom he met when she too was a mental patient at St Elizabeth's. Leslie was committed after she shot and killed her ten-year-old daughter and then attempted to commit suicide by shooting herself.

Hinckley and his girlfriend go out regularly. People complain that he lives a more privileged life than many who are free. Many people wonder where is the punishment for a man who inflicted so much pain on innocent people.

To this day Jodie Foster remains the victim of a stalker who was prepared to assassinate President Ronald Reagan, injuring three other people in the process, just to get her attention. It is easy to believe that Jodie Foster would find life a lot more reassuring if Hinckley was locked-up.

According to the law, however, John Hinckley, who many would see as a stalker with a lifelong obsession, 'is a patient, not a prisoner'.

CHAPTER EIGHT

The Material Man

Legislation in Los Angeles defines stalking as:

> '... the wilful, malicious, and repeated following or harassing of another person, which includes a credible threat with the intent to place that person in reasonable threat for his or her safety or the safety of his or her immediate family.'

In 1995, a pop superstar found herself caught up in one of the most bizarre stalking cases in recent times. This woman is probably one of only a handful of international celebrities recognisable by her first name. She is controversial, brash, creative, sexy, annoying and innovative – all rolled into one. The world's press has closely followed everything she has done since her meteoric rise to pop stardom in the early 1980s. She has sold over 150 million copies of her albums worldwide. Her successes include ventures into television production, merchandising, acting and publishing. She is estimated to be worth at least $650 million. Her name is Madonna Louise Veronica Ciccone.

Silvio 'Tony' Ciccone was the son of an Italian immigrant from Naples and Madonna Fortin hailed from a French-Canadian family; both were devout catholics and they married in their hometown of Bay City, Michigan in 1955. Ex-Air Force officer Tony worked as a defence engineer with the Chrysler Company and his wife

Madonna stayed at home and raised their five children: Anthony, Martin, Madonna, Paula and baby Christopher.

Tragedy struck the Ciccone family in 1962 when Madonna senior was diagnosed with breast cancer, while pregnant with her sixth child Melanie. Treatment for the disease had to be postponed until after Melanie's birth but by then it was too late to do anything to save her life. Madonna spent her remaining time looking after her children as much as she could and trying to give them as normal a family life as possible. Young Madonna was only five years old when her mother died surrounded by her husband and six children.

As the first daughter and her mother's namesake, Madonna felt the loss deeply. She had constant nightmares and hated leaving the security of her home. Her view of the world was changed forever.

Tony Ciccone was a quiet intense man who had to work extra hard to cope with his six motherless children. He was a firm disciplinarian, who remained quite a distant figure in his children's eyes. He employed a series of housekeepers to help run the house but he also expected them all to pitch in and help. The television was strictly rationed in favour of attention to school homework and sweets and treats were rare.

In the absence of her mother, Madonna turned to her father, seeking his attention and approval. Rather than becoming the rebellious child one might expect, Madonna became a 'Miss Goody-Two-Shoes'. She was always the first of the children to finish her household chores and would accompany her father to early morning mass at the local Catholic church each day. At school she joined the choir and became a class monitor. She worked hard in class achieving a Grade 'A' average – all to please her father. According to Tony, she was his 'little lady'.

In 1966, when Madonna was just eight years old, her life changed radically yet again. The latest housekeeper, Joan, started to go out with Tony and they soon announced their intention to marry. The small child who had lost her mother so early now felt that she was losing her father to this woman and with it, her place in his affections. A stepmother was the last thing Madonna wanted and she felt betrayed by her father. To make matters worse, a half-sister Jennifer and half-brother Mario arrived within two years. Tony then decided to make a fresh start by moving from the house the children had grown up in, to a new colonial-style house in up-market Rochester, New York State.

The arrival of a stepmother, and a new brother and sister, changed Madonna from a helpful and obliging little girl to a difficult and demanding ten-year-old. From the moment Joan became involved with her father, Madonna actively scorned her. When they married she refused to call her 'Mom', as her father suggested. She fought with her about everything. When she was forbidden to wear make-up and 'skimpy' clothes to school, she would smuggle the banned clothes out of the house and change later in the day.

From being a quiet, diligent schoolgirl, she became the classroom extrovert at St Andrew's, her new school. She was always looking for laughs and attention but her natural intelligence ensured that her schoolwork wasn't affected by her new behaviour. She was a popular girl and had lots of friends and boyfriends. Her love of pop music and dancing became quickly evident. Each Saturday she attended dance classes, where she learnt jazz, ballroom and tap dancing. She entered as many competitions as possible and was devastated if she didn't win.

After St Andrew's, Madonna moved to West Junior

High in 1972. Here her dancing skills earned her a place on the junior cheerleading squad where, under her tutelage, the junior team got the crowd's attention, leaving the senior team largely ignored and very irritated by the precocious young Madonna. At graduation, Madonna was one of the top ten achievers in the school.

In Adams High School Madonna moved onto the senior cheerleading team. Again she was very a popular teenager and had lots of male admirers. But her true passions were starting to take a grip. Madonna joined the Adams High Thespian Society, where she played roles in their productions of *Pygmalion* and *Cinderella*. She also played Morticia in their production of *The Adams Family*. But it was at a school talent show that Madonna really stunned her High School peers.

Madonna wanted to enter and win the annual High School talent contest. After nearly 3000 performances on Broadway, the musical *Godspell* was playing to packed houses around the world. It was a pop and theatre sensation and provided the ambitious teenager with just the role she needed to make an impression. She chose the character 'Sonia', and picked the song *Turn back, O Man*. For weeks she practised singing the song and choreographing her routine.

On the day of the competition Madonna performed her sexy routine flawlessly and the polished, slick performance wowed the audience who roared and cheered and gave her a standing ovation. Madonna was in tears as she took the applause and adulation, revelling in the experience of being the centre of everybody's attention. That night, the Adams High audience got a glimpse of the theatrics and talent that the rest of the world would soon clamour to see. Madonna had found her calling.

Fifteen-year-old Madonna then enrolled with a ballet

school in Rochester. The school was run by Christopher Flynn, a flamboyant homosexual, ex-ballet dancer. He had a reputation as being a great teacher who employed sadistic tactics with his pupils. He would hit them with a stick to get them into the correct position and pinch their legs to force them higher. He was an abrasive and caustic individual who used humiliation to encourage his students. For someone like Madonna he was probably the only person who could teach her the hugely demanding discipline of ballet. She threw herself into the training, practising for two hours each night. She appeared oblivious to Flynn's sarcasm and verbal abuse. It only encouraged her to improve and gain his respect. Eventually they developed a friendship and Flynn introduced his young protégé to the wider Arts world, helping her to discover other cultural interests. They visited museums and art galleries and attended concerts together.

By the time Madonna entered her High School senior year she had stopped playing the class clown and had begun to work hard at her studies. She also showed a change of style. She no longer followed the season's fashions, instead creating her own style; wearing bandannas, overalls and boots. She gave up wearing make-up and became a vegetarian. At night, to her father's annoyance, she frequented gay clubs with Flynn where disco was becoming the new dance craze. To Madonna, dancing was a natural expression and something that made her happy. She also found herself attracted to gay men, who presented no threat, and loved hanging out with them. They too were outsiders among the conservative Rochester residents.

When Flynn suggested that Madonna apply for a place on a Dance Program at the University of Michigan, she jumped at the chance. Her High School teachers also recommended her to apply even though it meant that Madonna would leave High School before graduation. Flynn's influence helped Madonna get a full scholarship. Her proud but worried father acknowledged that is was a great achievement. He finally agreed that she could go to Ann Arbor but insisted that Madonna stay in a girl's dormitory. Madonna left family life, Rochester and Adams High School behind a semester before graduating. She never looked back.

Madonna was convinced that dancing was the way she would achieve fame. She was single-minded in her dedication to her classes and devoted her absolute attention to practising. She continued to enjoy a lively social scene in Ann Arbor, again frequenting the Gay Disco scene there, and dancing the nights away. However, she never let it interfere with her work.

In the summer of 1977 Madonna won a six-week scholarship to the Alvin Ailey American Dance Theatre in New York. She adored New York and felt she had found her spiritual home.

In the autumn, she returned to college even more impatient to get on with her life and find her true 'destiny', which she now knew was in New York. She wanted to hang out with her new friends who were just as keen to succeed in dance. After two years in college Madonna convinced the 'Pearl Lang Company' in New York to take her on as a dancer. She had had enough of college and was impatient to move on to the next stage of her life. Her mentor Flynn encouraged her to go and he drove her to New York.

Madonna moved into a run-down apartment on the Lower East Side. She took a part-time job at the 'Russian Tea Rooms' and another at a fast-food outlet to pay the rent while she danced. She regularly posed nude for artists and art students for $7 an hour – work she loved doing because she was proud of her svelte dancer's body. Her life was simple and Bohemian. She visited art galleries, read classic novels and lived on very little food.

It wasn't long before Madonna started to get impatient again. She felt that time was running out and she was no closer to achieving fame. She was fed up with the thought of three more years of dance practice before she could even join a major dance tour, let alone play a leading role. She told Pearl Lang, 'I think I'm going to be a rock star' and left for good.

It was 1979 and Madonna threw herself into the world of music. She spent a brief period in Paris, dancing and providing backing for the French pop star Patrick Hernadez who was hugely popular at the time. Deciding that there was nothing in the job for her she headed back to New York. Her parting words to Hernandez were 'Success is yours today, but it will be mine tomorrow'.

Back in New York, she learnt how to play the guitar, the drums and keyboards. She dedicated every spare moment to perfecting her technique. A boyfriend from that time taught her the rudiments of song writing. Once she discovered that ordinary everyday events and emotions form the building blocks for song lyrics, there was no stopping her. Madonna had always kept diaries recording her feelings about both the most trivial and more important moments. She searched her diaries for ideas and started churning out songs at the rate of one a day. She also joined various groups but they usually broke up due to artistic differences or Madonna left, unhappy with their slow progress. Madonna finally became the lead vocalist with her own group *The Millionaires*, later renamed *Emmy*.

It was while she was with *Emmy*, playing a gig at 'Max's Kansas City', that she was spotted by the woman who would be her first manager. Camille Barbone was an Italian-American lesbian, whose ambition in the music business was to manage the biggest rock star in the world. She immediately knew she had found that person in Madonna. She wasn't interested in her band, just the wild and wacky lead singer. Barbone offered Madonna a contract that would include $100 per week, a one-room apartment and a part-time job as a cleaner. She also got her a contract with Gotham Records.

Barbone became Madonna's second mentor. They were good friends but Madonna continually flirted with Barbone, teasing the woman whom she knew had fallen in love with her. Her gigs were more regular and she usually earned $800 per night. At these gigs, Barbone would try to impress visiting record executives by employing break-dancers to perform during her set or paying young girls to dress in Madonna's style. However, things still weren't moving fast enough, Madonna felt she was wasting time. She wanted fame and she wanted it immediately. She vented her frustrations on Barbone, who felt deeply hurt both professionally and emotionally. She knew Madonna wanted to leave her. She started drinking heavily under the pressure.

The relationship soured and the two women were constantly at loggerheads. Madonna started to secretly meet other record industry people. Barbone then lined up record scouts to hear her at a gig in the famous *Underground* club. There was talk of album deals but by the time Madonna came on stage all the A&R men had left. Madonna was furious and fired Barbone, terminating their contract immediately. Barbone was devastated. Her drinking became excessive. She had a nervous breakdown and left the music industry altogether.

Madonna finally got her record deal with Warner

Brothers. It wasn't a perfect deal. The label would offer little back up but they did provide an advance for a two-single deal. She recorded her first single *Everybody* and through her own efforts at publicity, she got a lot of play in New York clubs. In July 1982, it entered the dance charts, and a few weeks later reached Number 1.

Surprised at the success, the record company quickly signed her for an album deal. At last, Madonna could smell success, her American dream was finally at hand. The granddaughter of an Italian immigrant was going to be the biggest rock star in the world and everybody would know her name. This made life even harder for Barbone as everybody started talking about 'Madonna', the latest rock star. Everywhere she turned, newspapers were writing about her, the radio stations were playing her hits and even the billboards carried her picture. There was no avoiding her former protégé.

Madonna the debut album was launched in 1983. Containing the phenomenal hits *Holiday* and *Lucky Star*, it went on to sell more than nine million copies. She started to appear on television and was fast becoming a household name. The fledgling music channel MTV loved her street chic and her flamboyant videos, which were tailor-made for their hip young audience. Madonna surrounded herself with a hand picked team to help her take on the world.

Her next album *Like a Virgin* hit the shops in 1984. It had to be delayed as the sales of *Madonna* had shown no sign of slowing down and the label didn't want to miss out on any sales. When the album came out the songs *Like a Virgin* and *Material Girl* were huge hits around the world. There was no stopping her – Madonna was a household name, not just in the US but all over the world. The *Material Girl* had made it.

Madonna's chequered love life took a new twist around this time. Madonna had had a string of boyfriends since she was fourteen but none ever earned her respect. She tended to move on to the next boyfriend without much regret. Then, while she was making the video for *Material Girl*, Madonna met the first true love of her life, actor and party animal Sean Penn.

They didn't meet up again until 1985. At this time Madonna had managed to break into the movies and was in Los Angeles making the critically acclaimed romantic comedy *Desperately Seeking Susan*. Madonna and Penn, both just out of other relationships, started to date. Madonna was smitten with the rough, edgy Penn. She thought they were two halves of the same whole. Both were dedicated to their careers and unwilling to compromise in their choices regarding them. They had a tempestuous relationship, sometimes known as the fighting Penns, generally because of Penn's naked contempt towards the paparazzi that chased them constantly. Penn also loved the outdoors life and disliked Madonna's New York scene. He particularly disliked the gay scene that so fascinated Madonna and he didn't endear himself to her friends.

Nevertheless, on August 16, 1985, Madonna's birthday, the couple married in a cliff-top ceremony in Malibu. The press, always in hot pursuit, found the undisclosed venue and bombarded it with reporters and photographers. Helicopters flew at such low altitudes that the couple could barely hear each other as they exchanged their vows. All in all, the carefully planned wedding was very disappointing for Madonna. Even the guests didn't mingle; the actors from LA stuck to themselves, leaving the 'wacky' New Yorkers to their own devices.

The newly-weds soon decided to make a film together. *Shanghai Surprise* was fraught with problems from the outset. There were on-set fights between the director and Penn. Madonna worked hard for her part but it soon became apparent that she lacked real acting experience. At the box office, the 'comedy' failed to make anybody laugh and the movie, which cost $17m to make, grossed only $2m worldwide.

Long separations due to work commitments caused major problems between the couple. Penn's aggressiveness also began to irritate Madonna. The media circus that had followed them since the start of their courtship hadn't eased off. Penn grew to hate them even more and got into regular fights with them. He was also drinking heavily at this time and Madonna thought he was partying too much. When he was jailed for drunk driving Madonna had had enough. Ten weeks later, in September 1987, she filed for divorce. Penn tried to win her back by cleaning up his act for a while. They briefly reconciled but following an incident in their home, which neither will discuss, Madonna ended the relationship for good. Penn has since married the actress Robin Wright.

Madonna's career reached a new peak of commercial success in 1990. She played the femme fatale Breathless Mahoney in *Dick Tracy*. During filming, she enjoyed a highly publicized fling with its director and star, Warren Beatty. After the movie Madonna took her infamous 'Blond Ambition' tour on the road. This tour showed Madonna at her most controversial: with outlandish costumes and a mélange of sexuality, dance and religiosity. When coupled with her affair with Beatty Madonna and her 'conical breasts' were in the news constantly. The tour was recorded for her 1991 documentary film *In Bed With Madonna (Truth or Dare)*.

The nineties were to prove lucrative for Madonna's music career. Hits during the decade included the chart-toppers *Vogue*, *Hanky Panky*, *Justify My Love*, (which was banned on MTV for its sexually explicit video) *Rescue Me* and *This Used To Be My Playground*. She also launched her graphic and erotic book *Sex*. The book sold out within hours, required an immediate reprint and went straight to the top of the best-seller list. Once again Madonna was the topic being discussed in the papers and on radio and television shows around the world. Many people were criticising the book. Even her staunch allies, the feminists, voiced their anger feeling that Madonna had let women down by publishing such a book.

Madonna's unstoppable popularity is generally attributed to her ability to constantly re-invent her image and her music. Her enormous wealth and assets are attributed to her clever record deals and her acute business acumen. In 1992, she signed a multi-million dollar deal, with Time-Warner, which left her in total control of her recording and publishing deals under her own label 'Maverick'.

In an attempt to safeguard her privacy, Madonna had bought a home that doubled as a fortress. Her house, Castillo del Lago, was built by Bugsy Seigal, the *Mafia* gangster. The pink, castle-style mansion, sits perched atop a rocky outcrop on a spectacular site in the Hollywood Hills. The views from the property are impressive and it affords a one hundred and eighty-degree panorama of the city of Los Angeles. It now became the refuge of the increasingly security conscious Madonna. High walls, however, couldn't deter one man – Robert Dewey Hoskins.

Robert Hoskins came from Northern California and Oregon areas. His family lived in rural areas in both states and he was a relative stranger to city life. He was married with several children. It subsequently became known to police that Hoskins had been arrested and investigated a number of times for abusing his wife and threatening his children. West Valley police found out that Hoskins had a violent reputation and once got into a fight with a police officer in his home state. He had apparently tried to stab the officer as he was been arrested and law enforcement officers considered him a dangerous person and a possible threat to others. The ongoing scrutiny from the police in his home state had been one of the primary reasons why Hoskins had fled to Los Angeles.

He first started to communicate with Madonna in February 1995, by sending her a series of letters which he signed 'your husband, Bob'. The letters were often detailed, explicit and, generally, meaningless. Among the hundreds of fan letters, which Madonna received, they were quite unusual. As a result they were given some attention, predominantly because of their strange content. The people who dealt with the star's mail felt they were the work of a 'whacko' but were not unduly concerned that the author might be an imminent threat. Why Hoskins decided to choose Madonna as his obsession is anyone's guess and he has never explained the reason behind it. Her international celebrity combined with her wealth and power would offer some explanation for the attraction. The letters certainly indicated a delusional belief that he was having some sort of relationship with Madonna and may have even believed that the singer was interested in returning his affections.

John Myers, a Public defender who later became involved in defending Hoskins, provided more information about Hoskin's background:

'He was a transient, he had been a transient for a long period of time. At one point or another he did become heavily involved in alcohol and drugs and that led to his downfall.'

Rhonda Saunders, the Los Angeles Deputy District Attorney, has been involved in the prosecution of many stalking cases. She is even more specific about the threat Hoskins posed to society:

'He was extremely dangerous – he had a history of domestic violence. His ex-wife and his children were in hiding from him. He abused her. He abused the children. He had taken one of the children and thrown it down a flight of stairs and the child's arms had been broken. He told his wife that if she reported him to the police he would kill the other children in front of her.'

If Madonna's management team had known about the past record of the man, who signed himself 'your husband Bob', they would probably have taken a lot more notice of what he was saying. Madonna took her personal security very seriously and had armed guards positioned around her home at all times. She travelled with a large entourage that included a full complement of security personnel. Her real fear was for her daughter, Lourdes, and any possible kidnap threat against her.

On the afternoon of Thursday, April 6, 1995, a shadowy figure lurked in the grass outside Madonna's home. He'd been loitering close by for some time. He crept towards the property, taking things very slowly, always on the lookout for a security guard or someone else from the house. Seeing an opportunity he scaled a wall and made his way to a courtyard close to Madonna's living quarters.

He was carrying a wooden heart that he had made especially for her. He wanted to give it to her in person.

Basil Stephens, Madonna's personal bodyguard was startled by the figure suddenly approaching him. He said that the man was 'ranting and raving'. He was claiming to be Madonna's husband and demanding to know where his 'wife' was. Madonna's 'husband' was so deranged and delusional that when Stephens told him to get off the property he fired the bodyguard. As Stephens later testified, the man said:

> 'you can't tell me to get off my own property, he said, you're fired – you get off my property ...'

The man was Robert Hoskins. The bodyguard chased him away but Hoskins was not so easily deterred.

The next day, April 7, Hoskins returned to Madonna's home. This time he contacted the staff in the house via a call box at the gate. He spoke to Madonna's personal secretary Caresse Norman. Once again Hoskins declared his love for Madonna and threatened to kill her if he couldn't have her. He told Norman that he was Madonna's husband and he wanted to see her. When she refused to let him in he then threatened to slit Madonna's throat from ear to ear. He said that he would kill Norman, and anybody else that was in the house with Madonna, if he couldn't see his 'wife'. He also said that he wanted to see Madonna immediately and that he wanted to marry her on the spot. His desire to marry Madonna indicated that on some level Hoskins knew that he was not her husband. However, the delusion was strong enough for him to ignore this 'minor' detail as he repeated his demands to see his 'wife'. Whether Hoskins threatened to kill Madonna

or not the contents of the note he had left for her are
scarily clear. The main thrust of the note was: 'You're my
wife you'll be mine for keeps'.

Rhonda Saunders describes the note's content:

> 'What he wrote the note on was a religious
> tract called 'defiled', so what you have is a
> note saying I love you but in big black letters
> at the top of the note it says defiled.'

The 'love note' was as follows:

MaDNNA
To
Louise
Ciccone
I love you
Will
You
Be my
Wife
for
keeps
Robert
Dewey
Hoskins
over

He drew hearts around the words and on the other side
he drew more pictures and wrote:

Im very
sorry.
Meet

me
somewhair.
Love for
keeps.
Robert
Dewey
Hoskins

He also wrote 'Be mine. And I'll be yours.' and drew a circle around it. The religious tract on which the poem was written stated that people who wear inappropriate clothing should be punished and people who have sex outside marriage should be killed.

Later during the court case the defence argued that Hoskins was just a drifter and hadn't chosen the pamphlet deliberately. They maintained that he had found it in a rubbish bin and its contents and their seeming relevance was just a coincidence. As John Myers commented:

> 'My argument was that Mr Hoskins led a transient lifestyle and probably just picked up this pamphlet out of a trash can. It was sheer coincidence that it happened to be this religious sect leaflet that said defiled. I don't think it had any significance or that he purposely selected this literature. I didn't think that Mr Hoskins was sophisticated enough to do something like that.'

As he left the note behind, Hoskins began to walk away from the property. Unexpectedly, he encountered Madonna. She habitually cycled and ran around the lake below the house with her personal trainer. Hoskins was heading towards the front gate when he saw her. He froze and just stood watching her until Madonna was right in front of him. Madonna rode by very cautiously and her trainer got in between the two of them. She later described how scared she was by the way he looked at her. In subsequent interviews she was able to give a description that was exact enough to identify Hoskins.

Hoskins made no attempt to communicate directly with Madonna but just stood and stared at her. As with many stalkers, when the moment finally arrives when they come face-to-face with the object of their obsession, they can often freeze and forget for the present why they are there in the first place. When Madonna got back to the house, her staff told her that the man at the gate was the same man who had trespassed on her property the day before. When they showed her the 'love note', it scared her almost as much as his threats to slice her throat had. Basil Stephens also thought that Hoskins was an extremely dangerous threat. The police were called, but they were unable to locate the man that night or in the weeks that followed. At Castillo del Lago everybody thought that that was the end of the affair – they were wrong.

Seven weeks later Hoskins came back to Castillo del Lago. This time events took a violent turn. On the evening of May 29, Hoskins once more scaled Madonna's twelve-foot high fence and bent back one of the steel poles holding the wire fencing. He ignored a 'No Trespassing' sign and crept up to Madonna's front door and tried to look inside. He left the door and walked towards the swimming pool.

Basil Stephens found him a while later down by the pool. He confronted Hoskins at gunpoint. Hoskins shouted back, 'I love her, don't you guys understand'. Hoskins then tried to tackle Stephens, screaming that he wanted to see 'his wife'. He shouted that he had come home to see Madonna and that Stephens and the other security staff were just in his way. Stephens wanted to detain Hoskins until the police got there. Instead of trying to run away Hoskins completely disregarded his own safety and lunged at Stephens. He tried to grab the gun. The bodyguard felt that if Hoskins got the gun the crazed 'husband' would shoot him. Stephens fired once, hitting Hoskins in the left arm. The bullet didn't stop Hoskins who kept running forward. Stephens then fired another shot this time hitting him in the stomach. Hoskins fell down, shot and wounded. Stephens immediately called an ambulance. At first he thought he had killed Hoskins, but by the time the ambulance had arrived he was sitting up nursing his wounds. Stephens was shocked by the altercation and said, 'I'm sorry I shot you', to Hoskins. He allegedly replied 'No problem'. Hoskins was taken to Cedars-Sinai hospital for treatment.

Robert Hoskins was later arrested for stalking and making terrorist threats against Madonna and members of her staff. Robert Dewey Hoskins was ordered to stand trial in Los Angeles.

On June 1, Hoskins pleaded not guilty to felony stalking, three felony counts of making terrorist threats and one misdemeanour count of assault. During a preliminary hearing at which Madonna was not present, Hoskins was held on $150,000 bail until his August 29 arraignment.

As a public defender, John Myers prepared a defence for the impoverished Hoskins:

> 'I got on very well with Mr Hoskins. He understood what he was being charged with, he was able to help in the presentation of his defence. Our defence was that he was merely

trespassing on the property and that was it. I
felt he had been over-charged with the charges
of making terrorist threats and stalking. I have
to say that despite the fact that we got along
okay I felt that he was delusional. He told me
at the beginning of our relationship that he
was married to Madonna, and he seemed to
honestly believe that. He indicated where they
got married and that they exchanged vows.'

John Myers thought that Stephens overreacted and didn't
need to use his gun:

'For a start, the security guard was much larger
than Mr Hoskins, he was taller, he weighed
more. He was also trained in martial arts, self-
defence and so on, so I thought the shooting
was an overreaction.'

Eight months after the events at Madonna's home,
the case against Hoskins came to court. Madonna was
determined not to testify, at least in open court. She felt
that this would give Hoskins exactly what he wanted – to
be in the same room as her. But on December 21, 1995,
Judge Andrew Kauffman ordered Madonna to go to the
LA Criminal Courts Building on January 2, 1996, to testify
against Hoskins. Madonna's lawyer, Nicholas DeWitt,
argued that Madonna was too 'sick and tired' to go to
court, following a trip to the UK, and had a very tight
schedule ahead, working in Argentina on her new movie
Evita.

John Myers insisted that Madonna make a personal
appearance in the court, saying that his client had a sixth
amendment right to confront and cross examine any

witness against him. Judge Kaufman ruled that Madonna must appear in court or face arrest and $5 million bail. DeWitt argued that Madonna was prepared to have the charges against Hoskins dismissed, to avoid the trauma of a court appearance. The prosecution declined to drop the charges. As Deputy District Attorney for the prosecution, Rhonda Saunders was worried that any conviction she might get against Madonna's stalker, might be reversed if she did not appear in court and she encouraged Madonna to testify.

On January 2, 1996, the day Madonna was due in court, DeWitt filed a motion that Madonna give her testimony on videotape, or, failing this, that Hoskins at least be removed from the courtroom when Madonna appeared. DeWitt argued that the court was playing into Hoskins' hands, by demanding that Madonna appear in the same room with him. However, the judge insisted on Hoskins' right to face his accuser.

The next day on Wednesday, January 3, 1996, Madonna reluctantly went to court. She wore all black and looked severe and strained. She entered the court building via an underground car park, frequently used to escort prisoners to and from their court appearances. The celebrity witness was surrounded at all times by Marshals of the Court and bodyguards. The courtroom was full of reporters, although cameras had been forbidden. She appeared to be very subdued and nervous when she took the stand to give her testimony. When asked about her non-attendance at the earlier court hearing, she replied that she hadn't attended because she was afraid of Hoskins and did not want to give him the opportunity to see her up close.

Madonna then recounted how she had seen him on one occasion at her house. She was disturbed by the crazy look in his eyes and his general scruffy appearance. When she had been told about Hoskins' threats that he would kill her and everybody else in the house if he was not allowed to see his 'wife', she said she was really upset and had 'felt incredibly violated'. Madonna told the court that she had started to have nightmares that he had broken into her house and was chasing her.

The longer her testimony went on the less nervous Madonna seemed to become and the angrier she appeared to get. She told the court that she didn't understand why she had to come into court and testify. She said she had asked to have her testimony videotaped and couldn't understand why this wasn't possible.

When asked how she felt about being in court with Hoskins, Madonna closed her eyes and said:

> 'I'm sick to my stomach. I feel incredibly disturbed that the man who threatened my life is sitting across from me and he has somehow made his fantasies come true. I'm sitting in front of him, and that's what he wants.'

Throughout her seventy-five-minute testimony Hoskins calmly watched Madonna, only occasionally fidgeting in his seat. Madonna deliberately avoided looking at him, except when she was asked to identify him. Then she looked straight at him and said, 'He's wearing a white shirt'.

Madonna stated that she had been so terrified by Robert Hoskins that she had decided to sell Castillo del Lago. She said:

> 'I felt it was an attraction to negative energy and I would be a target if I stayed in that

house. So I have put the house on the market
and I have decided to stay away from Los
Angeles.'

Next day in court Basil Stephens and Madonna's
personal secretary, Caresse Norman, testified. On January
5, Andy Purdy testified that he had given Madonna a
note that Hoskins had written. Purdy said that when she
read it she shuddered, '... like a cold chill had gone through
her body'. Madonna told Purdy that Hoskins made her
'...afraid for her personal safety' and she had rearranged
her schedule in order to spend more time in New York,
to avoid the possibility of ever seeing him.

In his closing arguments, John Myers attacked
Madonna, calling her 'a prima donna'. He claimed that
she could never stop acting. He accused her of being '...an
outright liar'. His defence had always been that Hoskins
was merely trespassing on the property. He maintained
that Hoskins had been over-charged with the terrorist
threats and stalking charges. He told the jury that Hoskins
was still supporting his children. According to Myers,
Hoskins was not the dangerous man depicted by the
prosecution.

The prosecution, on the other hand, maintained that
Hoskins was extremely dangerous and recounted his
history of domestic violence. Rhonda Saunders also pointed
out that the press had made a comedy out of Madonna's
ordeal. She thought that this had undermined her efforts
to bring attention to the real dangers involved in such
potentially violent cases. Saunders felt that being the target
of a dangerous stalker had taken a psychological toll on
the singer. She thought that Madonna would probably
continue to be threatened and frightened even if Hoskins
was jailed. She added that since stalkers are eventually

released, the victim must always worry about them showing up again.

On January 8, the jury, of eight men and four women, spent four and a half hours deliberating. They eventually found Robert Dewey Hoskins guilty of all five charges: one count of stalking, three counts of making terrorist threats and one count of assault. According to one juror who spoke later:

> 'As far as the women jurors were concern-
> ned, there was no doubt. The men took
> a little convincing on what would scare a
> person.'

John Myers asked for leniency for his client. He requested a sentence of five years and four months explaining that Hoskins had had a troubled childhood and suffered from a mental illness. In 1989, he had suffered a back injury that prevented him from working. Myers also pointed out that Hoskins was the only person who was physically harmed in the affair and his sentence should be based on what actually happened at Madonna's home not on what could have happened.

The prosecution, led by Rhonda Saunders, asked for a sentence of ten years and six months. Judge Connor agreed and rejected Myers' plea. Commenting on Hoskins' apparent mental illness, Judge Connor said, 'It doesn't decrease the danger, it appears to increase the danger' of putting him back on the street earlier. She also voiced her concerns about Hoskins' '...pattern of violence' and his '...extraordinary persistence and aggressive efforts'. She imposed a sentence of ten years. She further recommended that Hoskins serve his time in a prison with psychiatric services and fined him $200, which she said he could work off in prison. Hoskins showed little emotion as the judge passed sentence.

Madonna's attorney, Nicholas DeWitt, told the assembled press that Madonna hoped the judge's ruling would send out a message that '...society will not tolerate these types of threats' and of the verdict she said, 'it proves the system works.'

After the trial Madonna claimed to still have nightmares about the incident. She started to wonder whether she was responsible for the whole affair as a result of some of her more overtly sexual, public relations events. She thought that 'freaks' like Hoskins could perceive these events as something completely different – something like an invitation. When the famous LA-based private investigator Anthony Pellicano heard about Madonna's stalker, his reaction did little to allay her fears. He felt that Madonna attracted this type of fanaticism. He commented:

> 'Madonna attracts a lot of crazy people. ... She
> goes out in public and likes to flaunt herself.'

Meanwhile, Madonna tried to get on with her life. She went to Buenos Aires to begin filming the musical *Evita*. She played Eva Peron and gave one of the finest performances of her career eventually winning a Golden Globe award.

Unfortunately, the Hoskins' incident is not the only stalking incident that Madonna has had to deal with. In 1999, Madonna and her daughter Lourdes were given a police escort off a British Airways Concorde at Heathrow. British Airways' officials had received a call threatening action against Madonna when she arrived in Heathrow. Six police officers surrounded Madonna, who cradled her daughter in her arms, as she left the aircraft. There was no incident.

Another obsessed British fan, who has stalked Madonna for ten years, was warned by police that he will be charged and face jail unless he leaves her alone. Detectives wrote to thirty-two-year-old Jacob Johnson informing him that Madonna had complained about his harassment. He had visited her West London home and sent 'offensive and alarming' material through the post. They told him that the maximum sentence, if he was convicted, would be five years. In March 2002, he was heard on radio boasting that he had followed Madonna to America nine times and bombarded her with love letters, flowers and chocolates. Johnson admitted that he's 'been chasing Madonna for years' and he had '…given her nice necklaces and rings… and posted a few things through the door'.

Robert Hoskins is still in prison. It appears that he keeps his Madonna obsession alive – he recently sent her a video threatening to kill her. During an appeal, he insisted to the judge presiding that there is nothing wrong with him. Later, he threatened everyone who'd been involved in prosecuting him. Rhonda Saunders heard about the continued harassment and contacted Madonna's representatives to let them know that '…the threat is not over'. Hoskins is due for release in 2004 but Saunders wants to keep him in custody. Saunders feels:

> 'This is a man who should not be put back on the street because he could hurt or kill someone.'